Joe Fulda and Betsy Sikora Siino

Maltese

Everything About Purchase, Care,
Nutrition, Behavior, and Training

Filled with Full-color Photographs
Illustrations by Michelle Earle-Bridges

BARRON'S

2 CONTENTS

MEET THE MALTESE: AN INTRODUCTION

Take a look into the bright, black eyes of the Maltese. Though you seem to find the sparkle of a decidedly contemporary sprite, that sparkle actually emanates from a very ancient soul with an innate understanding of the human species.

Live with a Maltese for any length of time, and you'll join an illustrious club of Maltese fanciers who can imagine themselves with no other canine companion. Indeed, you will come to understand why this small dog has commanded such a fierce loyalty from her followers for so many decades, so many centuries.

An Irresistible Toy

The Maltese is among the more glamorous of the American Kennel Club classification of dogs known as the *toy breeds*, and she is quite accustomed to being referred to as "the aristocrat of dogs." For many centuries, Maltese have been household pets to people of culture, wealth, and fastidious tastes, thus accounting

The Maltese is as regal as she is lively, and she will capture the hearts of anyone lucky enough to know her.

for the Maltese reputation for refinement, fidelity, and cleanliness. This timeless breed continues to enjoy such reverence today, and it presents much the same image today, as well. The Maltese coat is described in the official breed standard as covering the body "from head to foot with a mantle of long, silky, white hair." Whereas the modern techniques of caring for and preparing the coat for dog shows have added to its glamorous appearance, the ancient breed possessed many of the same characteristics that have been passed on to our modern version of this wonderful little dog.

For those of you who are becoming acquainted with the Maltese for the first time, you are in for a rare and delightful experience in dog keeping. I use the words *dog keeping* instead of *dog owning* because nobody truly *owns* a Maltese. In the following pages, I hope to convince you that the opposite arrangement regarding who owns whom may be more

MALTESE MEMO

Love of Miniatures

As soon as humans learned to breed domestic animals selectively for individual traits, including size, they set about miniaturizing larger, usually working, breeds of dogs to make them into suitable household companions—in other words, to make them into toy dogs. The result is a very popular family of dogs that possess physical characteristics and temperaments identical to those of their larger brethren, but in smaller, more convenient packages.

Take a look at the Pug, for instance. You will see her massive Mastiff-type cousins in both her face and her fearless demeanor. Were it not for her diminutive size, you could certainly imagine the Pomeranian, with her pricked ears, smiling face, thick double coat, and plumed tail that she carries over her back, pulling a sled through the Arctic like the sled-dog cousins from whom she was bred. You certainly don't have to guess where the delicate Italian Greyhound got her long, spindly legs and commensurate speed, or why the English Toy Spaniel and the Cavalier King Charles Spaniel have such a desire to chase songbirds on their daily walks. Pit a Toy Poodle against her larger cousins in the obedience or conformation show ring, and the only difference you are likely to notice is size.

We all come from somewhere and someone. The same goes for our toy breeds, many of which leave no secret as to their illustrious origins. Indeed, within the family of toys, we can see the entire history of dogs and their relationship with humans as the closest of companions.

appropriate. Those individuals fortunate enough to have been around a Maltese for any length of time usually agree that at some point in the relationship, they have the revelation that *they* are being owned by the dog. Though it is true that the humans in the equation pay for the care and comfort of the breed (there is an unusual emphasis on comfort), and though they more or less dictate the itinerary, all of this seems to be contingent on the "earliest possible convenience" of the Maltese.

So be warned: If you are someone who objects to being owned by a dog, if you don't like brushing dogs, if you tire easily playing dog games or talking to people about how beautiful and extraordinary your dog is, you probably are not the best candidate for being owned by a Maltese.

Development and Popularity of Toy Dogs

Before we delve into the epic story of the Maltese, let's take a look at the canine family to which the breed belongs: the family of toy dogs. We can understand why people felt compelled so many centuries ago to breed tiny dogs, but we don't always know how those

Choose a Maltese for a pet, and you will quickly learn what it means to be owned by a dog—and a tiny dog at that.

first toys came about. Indeed, if the exact origin of the Maltese is questionable, the ancestry of many other toy breeds is a total mystery.

In 1981, noted author and internationally respected dog-show judge Maxwell Riddle wrote the book *Your Family Dog,* in which he stated:

> Giantism has been a way of life for many species ever since life on earth began. But as though in revolt against it, man has dwarfed many things, including cherry trees, cattle and dogs. Many of the toy breeds represent dwarfs of other dogs, but some have been dwarfed so long that no one truly knows how they got that way or from what parent stock they came. Yet, the Chihuahua, at 1½ to 4 pounds, is as much a true dog as the 200-pound Saint Bernard. A few of the so-called toy breeds are not really toys anymore. For example, some pugs and many shih-tzus are really outsized toys at the very best.

Though the miniaturization of dogs began long before, in the sixteenth century, several toy breeds were recorded to have been favored by the English royalty. They were said to have been pampered and petted lapdogs with whom ladies of the court slept, ate, and went riding. Their popularity carried on into the seventeenth century, and an assortment of small dogs accompanied King Charles II to and from the palace throne room. Charles allowed dogs in his chambers and to attend meetings of state, and there is even some evidence that litters of puppies were whelped in his bedroom.

Not for Everyone

Despite such charms, the fact remains that toy breeds, including the Maltese, are not for everyone. Would-be dog owners are often naturally drawn to the convenient size and the cuteness factor of the toys. However, they must also evaluate their lifestyles and family members, which, taken together, may prove dangerous to so small a dog.

Even among the toys themselves, the Maltese is not for everyone. Coated breeds—or those, like the Maltese, whose coats need more than occasional attention—come with a greater degree of responsibility in terms of time, effort, and money. While the aesthetic characteristics of the Maltese are most appealing, the beauty of the breed may not be enough to hold the bond between person and pet together.

The Maltese Muse

So now we come to the Maltese herself. We're not quite certain how the Maltese came to be—or even where the process that made her who she is began. To chronicle the origin of the Maltese, one starts with an age-old question: Did the breed originate on the island of Malta (the typical story line, given the dog's name)? Or do its name and ancestry begin in the Sicilian town of Melita?

Considerable evidence exists to support both claims, but one fact is certain: The Maltese was depicted on ancient Greek and Roman works of art dating back to approximately 500 B.C. The scribe Strabo, writing in the early part of the first century A.D., stated, "There is a town in Sicily called Melita from whence are exported many lovely white dogs called *Canis Melitei*." During that same era, Maltese were recorded in existence on the island of Malta. The Roman governor Publius had a Maltese named Issa, of whom a poet of the time, Martialis, wrote in one of his epigrams:

Issa is more frolicsome than Cattula's sparrow.
Issa is purer than a dove's kiss.
Issa is gentler than a maiden.
Issa is more precious than Indian gems, and,
lest the last days that she sees light should
snatch her from him forever,
Publius has had her painted.

Though we may never know the full story of this breed, the earliest accounts emphasize its charms and attributes, which seem to have been a part of the Maltese from her earliest days. A number of ancient authors discoursed on the beauty, intelligence, and lovable qualities of Maltese dogs, among them Callimachus the Elder (about 350 B.C.), Pliny the Elder (50 A.D.), and Saint Clement of Alexandria (around the second century A.D.).

One of the more celebrated, and relatively contemporary, pieces written about the Maltese was penned in Latin by Dr. Johannes Caius, physician to Queen Elizabeth I, sometime around 1570:

There is among us another kind of highbred dog, but outside the common run those which Callimachus called Melitei from the Island of Melita. That kind is very small indeed and chiefly sought after for the pleasure and amusement of women. The smaller the kind, the more pleasing it is; so that they may carry them in their bosoms, in their beds and in their arms while riding in their carriages.

Toy breeds, for the most part, are scaled-down versions of larger canine types.

We humans have long been enamored of "miniaturized" dogs, resulting in the creation of these two beloved breeds: the Yorkshire Terrier and the Maltese.

As we see, then, the Maltese has long been a frequent subject for writers, who invariably drew attention to its small size. In 1607, Edward Topsell wrote that these dogs were "not bigger than common ferrets." Not a very flattering description, but two hundred years later, in about 1792, Linnaeus referred to them as being "about the size of a squirrel." Danberton, in his *History Naturelle,* wrote that "ladies carried them in their sleeve."

Artistic Focus

More interesting to many people than literary references—and also perhaps more precise— are portraits. The Maltese is a breed that has always attracted the attention of artists. For example, Sir Joshua Reynolds's 1763 painting of Nellie O'Brien includes an unmistakable Maltese companion, typical in many respects to those you see today. Sir Edward Landseer also featured a Maltese, but established himself a more competent artist than prophet when he titled the painting *The Last of the Race.* Clearly, Landseer thought that the breed was destined for extinction.

The undeniable truth of the matter is that the painter can capture the sparkle in the Maltese eye, while the writer can pen endless adjectives to describe the Maltese's diminutive size. The writer can further impress us with anecdotes about the wonderful temperament of this breed of dog and her countless brushes with history and historical figures. However,

It is no wonder that the Maltese has for centuries been an inspiration to artists and writers alike.

you must bond with a Maltese to truly appreciate the breed's value as a companion: a unique blend of enthusiastic energy and regal stature, as well as an uncanny knowledge of when to be fun and when to be elegant.

The Maltese's Toy Story

People have long pondered the origin of many dog breeds, and, as we have seen, the Maltese is no exception. It is known that the Maltese is one of the ancient breeds and probably the oldest of the toy breeds. The Maltese Club of Great Britain claims that traceable information can be dated back to 8,000 B.C. That's more than 6,000 years before Strabo and Pliny the Elder.

As with so many breeds, England's Queen Victoria was responsible for earning the Maltese many lifelong friends. The following story is well known to Maltese historians:

A man known only as "Mr. Lukey" found a pair of Maltese in Manila, Philippines, in 1841. Lukey paid an extremely high price for the dogs with the intention of presenting them to Her Majesty. During the long voyage of about nine months to England, the dogs were totally neglected, and the condition of their coats on arrival made it inadvisable to offer them as gifts. The pair was, however, bred with success and most breed aficionados agree that these two dogs were the ancestors of a majority of all Maltese living at present in Great Britain and the United States.

Maltese puppies learn at the tenderest age that their job, their calling, is to hold court in the midst of a human family.

The question of origin could be researched for centuries with no provable conclusion, but from all that I have learned, there seems to be a probable answer. I believe, and at least two other canine scholars agree with me, that the Maltese did, in fact, originate on the Isle of Malta. There is enough evidence to support the idea that the breed flourished and gained popularity there, but for the same reasons that dog popularity fluctuates today, Maltese numbers dwindled on Malta almost to the point of extinction. Somehow, though, like a spark from a forest fire that leaps from the inferno and is blown miles away to ignite another fire elsewhere, the breed resurfaced in Melita years later. It emerged with just enough impetus to cause the cultures of the day to depict the breed on pottery, in writing, and in other art forms, consequently "reinventing" the Maltese and sealing its fate.

Canine historians and Maltese fanciers of Great Britain have been researching dog lineage for a longer time than researchers in the United States, and some of their research suggests that the original Maltese came from somewhere in Asia, perhaps around 2,000 to 3,000 B.C. They have also determined that the stone carving of a toy dog uncovered by archaeologists during excavations in Assyria was definitely a Maltese dating from about 2,000 B.C. And though the Chinese have not granted permission for Western archaeologists to dig there,

A Maltese puppy typically finds herself the center of attention wherever she goes.

Most Maltese won't say no to inappropriate treats and table scraps, but they will live longer, healthier lives if their owners resist the temptation to offer these to their tiny pets.

The Maltese is usually game to participate in virtually any activity as long as she can be close to her family.

It's not unusual for those who live with Maltese to regard them as children—and thus never leave home without them.

they have learned that a bejeweled dog statue recently excavated in China is believed to be a Maltese, dating back to about 3,000 B.C.

Long Live the Maltese

Not only did Sir Edward Landseer's 1840 prophecy of doom about the Maltese's fate go unfulfilled, the Maltese "race" is thriving today and does not seem to be going anywhere soon. The breed did fade somewhat around World War I, but it appears that the risk of extinction is over. Indeed, the Maltese's ancient legacy seems safe and sound; today the Maltese enjoys just the right level of popularity (too much popularity can be dangerous to breed

Despite their somewhat clouded history, we do know that Maltese have been enchanting both royalty and commoners alike for centuries.

health and quality) and a healthy number of AKC registrations.

The exact origin of your little "white-mantled" friend may be somewhat obscure, but that means little to anyone who has been close to the Maltese. Throughout the ages, in homes where the Maltese has resided, wonderful memories linger of a glamorous imp; a volatile, but good-natured family member; a frolic-loving, people-pleasing companion, who, by any standard, is the quintessential "good thing" in a small package.

Dog-show folks know the Maltese as a for-midable competitor. Men have found them-selves enamored of the breed's outgoing, fun-loving heart, something they never expected from a pampered toy. Intruders have discovered the Maltese to be a courageous and alert ankle-biter. And everyone else has enjoyed the company or even just the appear-ance of the Maltese. Whatever the circum-stance, encounter a Maltese and rest assured the incident will be memorable—you'll probably end up wanting one of your very own.

UNDERSTANDING THE MALTESE

Before taking the plunge and bringing a Maltese into your home and heart, you may just want to get to know the object of your affections a little better. You don't want to jump in blind, and it's wise to find out what you may be getting yourself into.

Maltese Character

The Maltese has very set opinions about life. What seems to suit his human in the way of comfort usually suits the Maltese as well. This is an ideal breed for elderly and solitary people, for apartment dwellers, and for quiet house-holds, but I have also seen Maltese thrive in a home where four growing, active boys were being raised.

This dog is not exactly enthusiastic about changes in routine, untidiness, or being set apart from a family gathering. Because of his small size, the Maltese is not typically the ideal dog for toddlers. However, if children around

Getting acquainted with the unique Maltese character will help to ensure a long and rewarding relationship with this spirited little dog.

him understand the word *gentle*, and have been well schooled in dog-play protocols, the Maltese can be a wonderful playmate with proper adult supervision.

The Maltese can also enjoy rousing games with other dogs, including much larger canine playmates. The obvious difference between a Maltese and other breeds is that the Maltese is probably going to be smaller and whiter than his playmates. Beyond that, your little friend is all dog. Because of his size, the Maltese cannot leap tall buildings in a single bound, but he can do just about anything else his larger four-footed, fur-bearing canine cousins can do.

The Committed Companion

Maltese mature slowly; it has been said that the Maltese remains a puppy longer than any other dog, thus earning the breed the label

The Maltese has had many centuries to perfect the breed's reputation as an ideal companion.

assurances and a consistent pattern of behavior on your part, indicating to the dog that you will return soon, go a long way toward establishing an everlasting bond. And this has nothing to do with gender. There is virtually no difference in temperament or affectionate responses to people between the male and the female Maltese. Both are equally affectionate, with clean toilet habits when properly trained, and both have the potential of being lovely, well-mannered companions.

"perpetual puppy." So if you're looking for a couch potato canine, this may not be the right toy for you. Despite his diminutive size, the Maltese enjoys all the fun activities associated with people/canine relationships, like going for walks, learning tricks, and playing any sort of "doggy" game his human family can think up. He is a curious, intelligent, adventurous, and very demanding package of energy and friendship, quiet and sensitive if that fits the mood of his human companion, or dynamic and playful should that be appropriate.

If there is a word that describes all Maltese, it would be *adaptable*. Yet at the same time, these dogs do not appreciate being wet, and they despise extremes in temperature. The Maltese is very responsive to his environment, and thus requires great understanding from his family regarding his preferred *comfort zone*. You can, for example, assume that your pet will not be pleased when left alone, but gentle

Potential Problems

Because the Maltese is such a cute and marketable commodity, he is often bred for the wrong reasons. In striving to understand the breed, one must consider potential problems—both genetic and those that can affect every dog—as well as the breed's character.

The Maltese, like other dog breeds, will be a non-tax-exempt dependent of his owners for 12 to 15 years and, all in all, should experience relatively few health problems when given proper care. Veterinarians have reported some cases of heart murmurs in Maltese, and I also would recommend that, during your pet's annual physical examinations, you ask your veterinarian to check your dog for shunt liver problems. Also, be sure to check the inside of your dog's ears regularly. Those long, heavily feathered ears make the Maltese susceptible to yeast or bacterial infections, but if you keep the ears clean and dry, you'll stay about 90 percent ahead of all ear problems.

Despite his diminutive size and long, flowing coat, the Maltese requires regular activity that challenges his mind as well as his small physique.

Keeping on Top of the Bottom

A Maltese owner must also pay particular attention to "rear end" cleanliness. Puppies especially should be inspected on a regular basis for any fecal matter that gets caught in the "potty-pack" hair. If excrement lodges in the hair and goes unnoticed, within a very short time it could block easy elimination and cause serious problems. Also, if you notice that your Maltese is scooting his rear end across the floor or remaining in a sitting position for extended periods of time, your dog may be attempting to express his anal glands, which are located just inside the anus. The biological function of these glands is to secrete liquid that lubricates the anus for easier elimination. If these glands are blocked, consult your veterinarian immediately. You can attend to this matter yourself by manually expressing the anal glands, but it is wise to have a veterinarian teach you the proper way to do it.

When properly socialized to other pets, the Maltese can learn to regard them as family.

Tear Stains

Perhaps the most bothersome of Maltese problems is tear staining, which occurs from runny or weeping eyes that stain the white

A well-bred Maltese is a picture of good health, proper conformation, and sound temperament.

unchanged for nearly forty years. Still, occasional improper ear sets, eye shapes, and slipped patellas (knee joints) have been seen in even the most carefully bred Maltese.

Fortunately, there has not been a tendency toward unstable temperaments in well-bred, properly nurtured Maltese, and because of its small size, the breed has remained relatively free of serious bone and hip dysplasia problems. Lifestyle can, however, lead to related problems. A new Maltese owner should bear in mind the size of a Maltese (about 8 inches [21 cm] at the withers). If allowed to jump from chairs, a Maltese will do so without fear, but he could injure his back, neck, and legs or tear ligaments in the process. Train your Maltese not

hair beneath the inside corners of the dog's eyes. This may be the result of sinus infections, allergies, dental problems, or eye abnormalities such as entropion, a condition where the eyelashes grow inward and irritate the eyes. Whether runny eyes are caused by age or the physical condition of the dog, they should be treated, if for no other reason than to rid unsightly, red-to-brown staining from under your pet's eyes and down the face. If allowed to go uncorrected, tear staining can result in skin problems and more serious conditions.

Other common problems associated with the Maltese breed are a low tailset and undershot lower jaws, which, because of some strange alignment of recessive genes, can crop up in the best breeding programs. Of course, conscientious breeders try very hard to eliminate these problems and produce puppies that conform to a breed standard that has remained

Never allow your Maltese unsupervised access to your furniture. A fall or jump could result in serious injury.

to jump on or off furniture, and you'll be protecting him from possible injury.

The Maltese Family Member

When you first bring your new Maltese into your home, you'll want to do your best to maximize his health and welfare while maintaining your own domestic tranquility. Here is an overview of what you'll want to avoid:

• Overstimulation: Excessive handling or an introduction to too many new sights, sounds, and activities too quickly can create stress and insecurity.

• Overfeeding or underfeeding: Poor feeding habits can cause diarrhea or malnutrition. Obesity can lead to a variety of health problems and substantially reduce the dog's life span.

• Lack of attention: Find the happy medium between overdoing and avoidance—too little attention can bring on anxiety and related behavior problems.

• Neglecting training: Start your housebreaking immediately to reduce accidents. Do the same with basic obedience to ensure your Maltese becomes a polite, confident—and safe—canine citizen.

• Taking a puppy to bed: You could roll on your puppy during the night and cause injury. Allow him to have his own secure corner of the world.

• Toys with bells, squeakers, or other small parts: Puppies can swallow or choke on bells or other toy attachments.

Children must be made aware that the Maltese's size makes it vulnerable to overly-rough play.

▬MALTESE MEMO▬

A Dog's Bill of Rights
Janet Mayer
(Excerpted from the July 1991
Dog Fancy magazine)

I have the right to . . .
• give and receive unconditional love
• a life that is beyond mere survival
• be trained so that I do not become a prisoner of my own misbehavior
• adequate food and medical care
• fresh air and occasional green grass
• special time with my people
• be foolish to evoke laughter
• earn trust and be trusted in return
• be forgiven
• die with dignity
• be remembered with love

The unexpectedly rugged little Maltese is a toy breed that is favored by men as well as women.

Don't expect too much, too soon from your new Maltese family member. Give him time to adjust to your lifestyle and his new environment. The Maltese is tiny yet hardy, but he doesn't respond well to rough handling and loud voices. Do everything right, and it won't take long for this small creature to adapt to his new household. He will start checking out your every move right away. Part of what a dog does best is to memorize the routines in his

You should begin to teach your puppy what is acceptable behavior—and what is not—as soon as he joins your household.

environment; it is an instinctive part of his natural survival package.

Survival Skills

Centuries ago, before their total domestication, puppies born in the wild quickly learned that survival depended on knowing every positive and negative aspect of their surroundings. This enabled them to better hunt for their food, to conceal themselves from danger, and to make maximum use of their habitat. Most animal behaviorists agree that a dog coming into a family of two or more people "locks in" on one member, seeming to prefer the company of that person over the other family members based on a combination of elements. In a canine evaluation system, the questions that must be answered are: Who feeds me? Who plays with me or gives me the most attention? Who protects me? If Mom feeds the dog, Junior or Sis gives him the most attention,

and good old Dad seems to be the logical candidate for protector, your dog's preference will be based on his individual priorities.

Indeed, one dog may prefer the company of the person who feeds him over the companionship of the others. If eating is more important to the dog than playing or his own security, then it is quite natural for that dog to bond closely with the human who provides the kibble. Close observers of the Maltese would argue, however, that the breed is versatile and flexible with all family members, developing a special relationship with each member of the clan.

Communicating with Your Puppy

Dogs communicate with each other by scent, body language, and eye contact. Through their sense of smell, which is a thousand times more sensitive than that of humans, dogs determine

Your Maltese will look to you for both verbal clues and body language to understand where he stands in the family pack.

the sex, temperament, and intentions of every dog they encounter. Dogs also use body language to convey their own attitude, temper, and intent to others, as well as to advertise their particular position in the pack. The way the ears are carried, a slight movement of the lips away from the teeth, the tensing (or relaxing) of the body, and the position of the tail are all signs that can be interpreted by other dogs. Another sign is the band of hair that runs down the middle of the back, which will stand upright or bristle when a dog is angry or assuming a defensive posture. This "puffing-up" is intended to give the impression of greater size and formidability.

Eye contact is another important means of communication for dogs. A direct stare is a challenge in dog language, whereas averting the eyes indicates a desire to avoid confrontation; an aggressive dog should never be stared at directly. It is, however, very rewarding to meet the eyes of a dog who thinks you are the greatest thing in the world. The softening and almost smiling message in the eyes of a devoted dog is a measure of love that's hard to duplicate.

Maltese are not at all different from other dogs when it comes to their fluency in canine language, and it is a clinically proven fact that dogs—all dogs—are *pack oriented*. That is, canine perception has a great deal to do with pecking order, and each member of the pack must learn his or her position in the family group. In the average family situation, your dog will likely look upon the dominant or most assertive human as the pack leader.

We have all seen households that seem to be dominated by the family dog—even a dog that weighs in at 7 pounds and is nothing but a ball of white fluff. It's not a pretty sight. But teach a dog his place gently and with love, and you do everyone a favor. If a dog knows that his position is recognized and accepted by the other family members, who in turn treat the dog with respect and consistency, you can all live happily ever after.

The Crate: A Place of His Own

One area of controversy over the years has been the issue of putting dogs in crates, those airline-type shipping containers or kennel enclosures made of wood, fiberglass, reinforced wire,

Every Maltese's greatest wish is to be a valued, beloved member of the family.

or metal. Some behaviorists have been critical of crating, and their objections may certainly be well-meaning. However, in my estimation, crating is a method of management that most dogs come to enjoy and appreciate. The idea goes back to the natural habitat of wild dogs a thousand years ago, when dogs were den or cave dwellers and sought private places far from the paths of other animals and humans.

Crating is appropriate for the Maltese because of his small stature. In a crate, with a door not necessarily closed, little dogs avoid many risks. Indeed, most dogs—and homes—are safer if the dogs are confined when their owners are not at home. Puppy accidents, such as chewed slippers or electric cords, are more easily avoided if the dog is confined when you are away. In addition, dogs placed in crates or similar confinement when they go to a veterinary hospital will likely experience less stress if they have become accustomed to being in a crate at home.

Crating also aids in housetraining because dogs do not usually relieve themselves where they sleep. Most adult Maltese are able to "hold it" for six to eight hours without any trouble while an owner is working or sleeping. Crates are also convenient doghouses when you are traveling, both for a safe drive and a safe and pleasant stay when you arrive at your destination. Hotels, motels, and even out-of-town family friends are far more receptive to dog owners if they know the dog will be confined to a crate

in the room. An investment in a crate is small compared to cleaning or replacing a carpet or, worse, paying a veterinary bill to repair a broken Maltese leg. All things considered, a Maltese in a crate is safer, and so is your home.

A crate can be your Maltese's private place, can help simplify training, and make travel safer and less stressful for the dog.

YOUR FIRST MALTESE

So you've decided that you want to be owned and manipulated by a Maltese. If you are one of those people who always has your ducks lined up on the pond, you'll no doubt want all the information about Maltese that you can absorb. Of course, you've already taken a big step in discovering Maltese by acquiring this book. Reading all you can about your breed of choice may be the first positive step in understanding the best ways to care for a dog.

By all means, before you acquire a Maltese, speak to Maltese owners, speak to reputable breeders, and learn the breed's standard. Do this, and you'll be prepared to make a wise, informed decision.

Wise Decisions

An important ingredient in selecting and caring for a dog is common sense. More people are inclined to care for—and choose—a pet from the heart than from the brain. Use that brain of yours to consider all the consequences before you take the plunge. Begin with the details. Whether acquiring a full-grown adult or a Maltese puppy, consider any limitations

A joyful day it is when a new pet Maltese joins the family.

that might be imposed on your relationship by your lifestyle. If you live in an apartment, for example, providing your puppy with daily exercise and waste elimination will be an adjustment you'll have to make.

Puppies are undeniably irresistible, but when acquiring one, you must also visualize the full-grown dog that puppy will someday become. You should consider what it takes to shepherd that adorable puppy toward becoming a beautiful, well-adjusted adult Maltese. In addition to meeting as many Maltese as you can, you might find it helpful to review the American Kennel Club's breed standard for the Maltese. Every quality purebred dog is bred to a blueprint, or standard, that describes the ideal specimen of that breed. It includes a detailed description of the anatomy and the characteristics of the breed. Once you know

MALTESE MEMO

About the Maltese Standard

The American Kennel Club breed standard for the Maltese (as approved by the national breed club, the American Maltese Association) calls for a dog of 4 to 7 pounds that is covered with "a mantle of long, silky, white hair." His tail should be a "long-haired plume carried gracefully over the back," and he should sport "drop ears" that are "heavily feathered," as well as eyes that are "very dark and round, their black rims enhancing the gentle yet alert expression." He should move with "a jaunty, smooth, flowing gait," his straight, pure-white coat flowing almost to the ground.

Also of importance are the standard's mandates on Maltese temperament. The Maltese should be "gentle-mannered and affectionate," yet "eager and sprightly in action, and, despite his size, possessed of the vigor needed for the satisfactory companion." The Maltese should seem "to be without fear." In sum, he is "among the gentlest of all little dogs, yet he is lively and playful as well as vigorous."

You can see, then, how the standard offers would-be Maltese buyers a clear picture of who this dog is meant to be. Armed with this knowledge, you will be far better prepared to choose your new companion with a clear and informed head. (For the complete Maltese breed standard, contact the AKC at the address included at the end of this book.)

the breed standard, and have tried to meet some real, live Maltese, you are ready for the next step: finding the Maltese of your dreams.

Where to Purchase Your Puppy

Though an ethical, reputable breeder is the optimum source for a Maltese puppy, it's not the only source out there. For obvious reasons, you should never acquire a puppy from someone in whom you cannot place full confidence. You are wise to avoid "backyard breeders," amateurs who are just out to make a few bucks off the family pet or to create a project for the kids. Stick with a reputable breeder.

The Reputable Breeder

Just what is a reputable breeder anyway? A reputable breeder is a person who has studied all aspects of the breed in question, who will help educate potential buyers, and who will give the breed's image and the enhancement of its good qualities the same high priority as finding proper homes for his or her puppies. In short, the reputable breeder is someone who has devoted his or her life to the breed, someone who breeds out of love rather than for the promise of monetary gain.

A reputable breeder will tell you honestly about any undesirable characteristics or problem areas related to the breed and challenges you may face as an owner—perhaps the challenge of caring for the beautiful Maltese coat. When contacting a Maltese breeder, ask such questions as, "How long have you been breeding Maltese?," "What got you into breeding Maltese?," and "What recognized dog organizations do you belong to?" Every AKC-recognized

Choose your new Maltese pet with your head as well as your heart.

breed has its own national breed club devoted to the promotion of its breed and the ethical conduct of its breeders. Nearly all reputable breeders are affiliated in some way with their national clubs, as well as kennel clubs, breed-rescue groups, and other responsible owner/breeder organizations.

In this day and age, most breeders—reputable and disreputable alike—advertise and promote their operations on Web sites. Via the Internet, you may find breeders who are not close enough to permit your personal inspection of their facilities and puppies. Many a fine puppy has come to its new family in this way with very positive results, yet some words of caution are in order. While the Internet may provide you with a good introduction to a breeder and his or her dogs, purchasing sight unseen from the Internet can be risky.

The major reason most buyers work with reputable breeders is rooted in their reason for acquiring a purebred dog in the first place: predictability. Meeting the sire and/or dam of a litter gives you a pretty good idea of what the little ball of fur cavorting around your feet and tugging at your shoelaces will look like, and even act like, in a year or more. With Internet puppies, you may see the parents of the litter only in photographs, and you cannot observe how the puppies are being raised. If you are purchasing a puppy this way, you should ask for and receive guarantees that your puppy is completely free of genetic problems, and that you may return the puppy if there is a problem or you are for some reason dissatisfied. Call me old-fashioned, but the idea of buying a dog

sight unseen has never appealed to me. Nevertheless, some pretty respectable dog breeders offer puppies for sale this way—just remember to ask for and receive clear guarantees before, during, and after the sale.

Alternate Sources

Depending on the type of Maltese you are looking for, I would strongly encourage you not to overlook the possibility of finding your perfect companion at the local animal shelter or through a Maltese breed-rescue group. For any number of reasons (the kids were too young and disrespectful, the owner died, etc.), perfectly wonderful purebred dogs are often abandoned or given up to shelters and pure-bred breed-rescue groups. Every day these organizations find themselves fostering little treasures just waiting to be wonderful pets. But choosing such a puppy is no different from choosing from a breeder. Ask questions, and remain on guard with your common sense.

The Maltese's AKC breed standard describes the classic Maltese coat as "a mantle of white."

Locating a Reputable Breeder

Let's say that you have decided you would like to work with a breeder. Where do you find this person? An excellent source for this information is a veterinarian because reputable breeders (and responsible owners) have a family veterinarian as sure as they have a family physician. Many veterinarians own purebred dogs themselves—some are even breeders and dog show exhibitors and judges—so on all fronts they are plugged in to the local kennel-club set.

Which brings us to the next logical source of information: the local kennel club, which, with any luck, boasts local Maltese breeders as members. In case you live in a town that doesn't have a dog club, you can contact the American Kennel Club for referrals to canine organizations in your area. Grooming shops are also obvious sources of information for finding breeders of this coated toy breed, as are local boarding kennels.

Once you have collected names and information, visit kennels advertising Maltese for sale. Clean facilities will give you the first good impression that you are dealing with a caring source. And remember, don't be shy about asking questions. A breeder's reputation depends on treating every client fairly, and respecting your questions is part of that. Good breeders will riddle you with questions, as well, to ensure their puppies go to the right homes with the right families.

Again, let common sense be your guide when evaluating breeders. If you find a Maltese

MALTESE MEMO

Questions, Questions

The American Maltese Association suggests that would-be Maltese buyers ask breeders the following questions:

✔ How long have you been breeding Maltese?

✔ How many other breeds do you have? (It's a real plus if Maltese is the one and only.)

✔ Do you insist that all non-show-quality puppies for sale be spayed/neutered at the appropriate age and not be allowed to produce puppies of their own?

✔ Do you offer in writing to take or buy the dog back, should this ever become necessary?

✔ What temperament problems might I encounter? Is this an easy breed to train and housebreak?

✔ Do you keep vaccine records on your puppies?

✔ What type of contract, conditions, or guarantees are involved in the sale of the Maltese puppy? (Reputable Maltese breeders will provide a written contract/guarantee with a spay/neuter requirement or AKC Limited Registration for pet-quality puppies. They do not sell breeding animals to pet homes.)

✔ Can you give me at least two references of people who have acquired your puppies in the past?

✔ Do you participate in the rescue of abandoned and owner-relinquished Maltese?

✔ Do you require that would-be buyers visit the premises where the mother and puppies reside so they can see how your dogs are raised and cared for?

✔ Are you licensed by the U.S. Department of Agriculture? (If the answer is yes, this is a red flag that the breeder may be running a puppy mill. Licensing is required by the USDA for any breeder who sells more than $500 of puppies to a broker or pet shop per year.)

✔ Do you have a "nonrefundable" deposit clause? (Most Maltese breeders do require a deposit, but there is no valid reason why it should be nonrefundable.)

breeder who suggests meeting you in a store parking lot, that's a major caution flag that this person is trying to hide something. You should always be welcome to see the living conditions of the Maltese puppies you are considering, as well as their parents. By the same token, beware of Maltese breeders who do not question you about your home and family situation, or how you intend to care for your new pet. They are more than likely concerned only about the financial aspects of the sale, and are not all that interested in providing the very best homes possible for their Maltese.

Breeder commitment and expertise may also be determined by asking specific questions that deal with the breed standard. A big red flag of caution should be running up the pole if you mention the breed standard and find yourself

Health Checklist

The following factors should be considered when evaluating puppies as potential pets:

✔ General healthy condition; alert, bright eyes; overall clean look and smell; a clean nose; clean ears and feet.

✔ Skin and coat: Rub fur against the direction it lies and look for red skin, bald patches, or flaking skin. Coat should be uniform and healthy looking.

✔ Observe the puppy walking and running, and look for abnormalities.

✔ Inquire about worming and vaccinations; by 14 to 15 weeks, the puppy should have had most, if not all, puppy shots.

✔ Ask to see the sire and/or the dam. Ask to see siblings if they are not present. Compare.

✔ Ask about registration papers.

If you can see the father of a litter, you can get a good idea of how the breeder's dogs look in top condition.

staring at a blank expression. Indeed, if you have any doubts as to the breeder's honesty or the veracity of any information he or she gives you, check it out—or move on. Remember, it is your right and responsibility to make your purchase from someone who takes all the steps necessary to produce dogs of quality and good health, and who stands behind what he or she sells. There can be no gray areas when it comes to selling living creatures. Defective Maltese puppies, unlike toasters or automobiles, suffer pain, as do the owners who love them.

AKC Registration

One more word of caution: The designation "AKC Registered" after the name of a kennel simply means that the kennel's name is protected for the sole use of its owner in naming dogs from that kennel to be registered or shown. When you buy a dog that has been represented as being eligible for registration with the American Kennel Club, you are entitled to receive a certified application form properly filled out by the seller, which, when completed by you and submitted to the AKC with the required fee, will register the dog. After the application has been processed, you will receive an AKC registration certificate. This certificate and the registration papers are not for sale (nor are they evidence of a dog's health or quality).

When purchasing a puppy, do not accept a promise of later registration. AKC rules and regulations stipulate that whenever someone sells a dog that is represented as registrable, the dog must be identified, either by giving the buyer a properly completed AKC registration application, or by giving the buyer a bill of sale (or a written, signed statement), stating the dog's breed,

A reputable, ethical, not to mention knowledgeable, breeder is worth his or her weight in gold when you are seeking a well-bred Maltese puppy.

sex, color, date of birth, the registered names of his sire and dam, and the name of his breeder.

The AKC has always recognized the role of the responsible breeder in preserving the integrity of its registry and the quality of purebred dogs in this country. In June of 1989, the club voted to give breeders a valuable tool to protect their programs: the option of selling their puppies under full or limited registration. Dogs with full registration privileges can compete in all AKC events, and their offspring can be registered with the AKC. Dogs with limited registration privileges are allowed to compete in all AKC Companion and Performance events, but not in Conformation events (dog shows). Additionally,

puppies produced by a dog with limited registration are not eligible for AKC registration.

The choice to register a dog with full or limited privileges is solely in the hands of the dog's breeder. The breeder indicates the full or limited designation on the dog's individual registration application. The breeder's designation is entered into the AKC registration system along with the dog's name, sex, color, and number, and it becomes part of the dog's permanent registration record. If the dog is entered in an AKC event, or if he appears as a parent on a litter application, this information is checked for eligibility against the dog's full or limited registration status.

AKC registration means only that a Maltese is a purebred, not that he is necessarily show quality or even genetically healthy.

What to Look For

If you think that researching and educating yourself about the Maltese and the people who breed them is a monumental effort, you'd better brace yourself. The most difficult task of all is at hand: the actual selection of your new pet.

Because the one common denominator for puppies is "cute," selecting a healthy puppy should be your primary concern. First, I do not recommend taking home a puppy that is younger than 8 weeks of age (12 weeks is even better). For stability in their physical and emotional development, puppies require sibling interaction, a good dose of TLC from mom, complete weaning from maternal dependence, and their first round or two of puppy immunizations. It is also easier for you to evaluate puppy temperament in a 10-week-old puppy than it is in a 6-week-old. And finally, at 10 to 12 weeks of age, puppies adapt to humans more readily than they do at a younger age.

Show Quality or Pet Quality?

Look for the healthy puppy, yes, but also for the pup you like and who likes you back. Here the breeder can be a big help. Discuss your lifestyle and what you envision your long-term relationship with your pet to be. Good breeders

Remember that a Maltese is more than just a pretty face. It's your job to evaluate your potential companion's health, quality, and temperament.

MALTESE MEMO

Maltese and Babies

Many Maltese believe that they are the babies of the family, and it can be a rude awakening to find a human baby brought into the fold. With proper preparation, training, and introductions, Maltese and baby—and ultimately Maltese and child—can become lifelong friends. You can help ease the initial transition by following the tips below:

✔ Before the baby's arrival, make sure your Maltese is current on his obedience training, both to strengthen the bond between dog and owner and to help fortify your control of your dog.

✔ Put a stop to such behaviors as biting or nibbling on hands or ankles. Provide plenty of chew toys instead.

✔ Introduce your Maltese to friends' babies and well-behaved children to accustom your pet to the actions and noises of young humans.

✔ Allow your pet to investigate a blanket or similar item that carries the baby's scent before you bring the baby home.

✔ With careful supervision, allow your Maltese to sniff the new baby upon his or her arrival in your home.

✔ Make sure your Maltese continues to get plenty of attention and exercise as you all adjust to the new baby, and reward him profusely for sitting or lying quietly beside you as you feed and tend the baby.

✔ Include your pet in daily walks when you take the baby out for a bit of fresh air.

✔ For the safety of all, never leave the dog and the baby (or any child) alone and unsupervised.

know their puppies, and they can help guide you in making a perfect match.

A common misconception exists among the general public that because a dog is registered with the American Kennel Club or some other canine registration body, it is a show-quality canine. This is not true. Registration papers simply document the fact that the parents (both sire and dam) were issued registration numbers and that their parents and grandparents were registered, and so on. The basic principle of registration makes it possible to track the heritage of a purebred and to assure new owners that their acquisition is indeed a purebred.

What's the Difference?

The term *show quality* is intended to describe a purebred dog with attributes that, when judged by a competent and acknowledged authority, conform to what is considered to be an ideal specimen of the breed. A registration certificate cannot guarantee the dog's quality, only the fact that the dog's parents were also registered purebreds. In fact, there is no guarantee that because a puppy's parents were champion show dogs, the puppy, too, will be fit for a successful show career. In fact, more often than not, out of a litter of five puppies with the sire and/or the dam as dog-show titleholders,

The best breeders are as proud of their pet-quality puppies as they are of their puppies destined for the show ring.

only one or two of the puppies might turn out to be show quality. Sometimes even the most carefully matched breeding does not produce one show puppy in the litter.

But don't write off the breeder's pet-quality puppies. They may not meet the nuanced ideals of the breed standard apparent only to a veteran show-ring judge, but they are beautiful nonetheless and, like their show-quality siblings, are the products of the same high-quality breeding program. Show- and pet-quality alike, I firmly believe that when a dog, any dog, is well cared for by a loving and responsible family, the role of protector, companion, and champion of your backyard is just as important as satin ribbons or shiny trophies. Show quality is great, but it must always take second place to a dog's role as beloved family member.

Bringing Your Maltese Home

If you've made the right preparations, the trauma of a dog's transition from one environment to another can be greatly reduced. There are always going to be adjustments for the dog, but dogs are adaptable creatures when their basic needs are met by sensitive, well-prepared owners. If your new pet has nutritious food, comfortable shelter, clean water, and properly measured attention, it will take only a short time for him to settle into your routine.

So what preparations should you make before your new Maltese comes home? First, figure out where your new pet will be sleeping. Set aside a quiet corner of the house that can be his private, comfortably appointed sanctuary, even if he will be trained to view a dog crate as his bed.

Next, take a trip to your local pet supply store for supplies. To begin, you will need:

✔ Food and water dishes.

✔ An appropriately sized buckle collar and, if possible, current identification tag (which the puppy, then dog, should wear at all times).

✔ Safe chew toys.

✔ A dog crate.

✔ A lightweight leash or lead (nylon or leather, no chain).

You will also need food. You've just made a new friend, and it's your job to convince that friend that his new environment and family are going to be even more comfortable and loving than the ones he just left. Food plays an important role in that mission, as stress can have a profound effect on appetite.

Advice on what to feed should begin with the former caregiver, who can provide information on your new dog's eating habits and every other element of his life to date. The more information you have about where your dog has been, the easier it will be to bond with your new pet and overcome any problems you might encounter while establishing that bond.

Preparing a Training Game Plan

Training plays a critical role in helping a puppy adjust to his new home and bond to his new family. Maltese are happiest inside the home and close to their families—their coats were not designed by Mother Nature for retriev-

When lifting a puppy, place one hand under the hindquarters and the other hand under the chest and abdomen.

ing birds in the underbrush. You will probably prefer to spend time with a dog who knows how to behave within the household. At the same time, your dog will appreciate a mechanism by which he can feel secure and confident. Training will satisfy both goals. While we will delve deeper into training in a later chapter, keep in mind now that it's never too early to introduce your new Maltese to the concept.

Understanding the Maltese philosophy is an important step toward beginning your training regimen: "Close to you is good, closer is better, and consistently close is best." In establishing this closeness and your dog's sense of security without giving up your control of the foot of the bed, provide a space that belongs exclusively to your Maltese. A dog crate fills this role; when your Maltese adjusts to his home-inside-the-home, he will begin to view himself as a bona fide landlord of that domain. Once

Puppies, like human children, crave boundaries, so begin training your Maltese puppy as soon as he crosses the threshold into his new home.

the crate has been established and accepted, leave the door open so your dog can come and go as easily as you enter and exit your house. Dogs can even learn to take their meals inside the crate, and you can purchase attachments that hold water and food bowls. Don't be too surprised to find your dog's toys piled up in the crate as well.

Housetraining Your Maltese

Now that you have all you need to make your puppy feel at home, one of the most important stages of training begins: the dreaded task of housetraining. Of course, you need not dread housetraining if you commit to it properly. Remember that the Maltese is a

fastidious little creature who tends to be a very cooperative and competent student once he understands the routine.

Establish an unwavering routine that fits your schedule, commit to close observation, follow a few simple rules, and housetraining can be accomplished in just a few days. Dogs are intelligent creatures. Their entire agenda is based on their need to please, and they figure out quickly that it is rewarding to please the source of their food and comfort. Scold gently when accidents occur, but remember: Just as you must offer positive praise immediately and on-the-spot to get best results, scolding at the very moment of indiscretion—not two hours or even two minutes afterward—is also necessary and effective.

The Rules for Housetraining

Follow these steps, and you may find that in no time you are living with a Maltese with impeccable bathroom habits:

1. Take the dog outside to a familiar location at regular intervals. Don't *put* the dog out. *Take* the dog out.

2. Suggested times for bathroom breaks are: first thing in the morning; immediately after each feeding, nap, and play session; and just before going to bed. Yes, you'll be going in and out all day long.

3. Observe your dog's body language. Dogs send "potty-alert" signals when they get interested in sniffing at certain spots, when they suddenly appear anxious or overly busy, and when they stand beside a closed door with an uneasy look in their eyes.

4. Encourage the dog with a short command like *"Go potty!"* When the dog relieves himself, heap large amounts of praise upon him. Let him know he has pleased you, and he'll look forward to doing it again.

Housetraining isn't nearly as difficult as its reputation paints it to be. And just wait: As your puppy matures, so will his urinary tract. The day will come when he no longer needs to run in and out all day long to relieve himself.

For most dogs, the housetraining routine is the first introduction to formal training, so try to remain positive and consistent. You will soon see how its tenets carry over to other training areas, as well. A dog who is praised when he does the right thing, and who is corrected firmly with tough love when he does wrong, will quickly learn acceptable behavior. In all training, you must be consistent. This means that certain actions by the dog are always prohibited, while others are always encouraged.

Whether you are housetraining your Maltese or teaching him basic manners within the household, remember that above all, your dog wants to please you.

All successful dog training is based on the three Rs: Routine, Repetition, and Reward. Adhere to the housetraining routine (or any training routine), repeat and review every phase of training, and then top it off with praise or, occasionally, a treat. Your personal reward from the housetraining regimen will come in the form of a strong bond between you and your dog, and, of course, the preservation of your carpets. Just remember that no matter how sharp your Maltese, a dog is not trained overnight, so supplement your efforts with a big dose of patience and perseverance.

FEEDING YOUR MALTESE

Just like their human counterparts, Maltese are what they eat. By instilling proper eating habits in your puppy—and proper Maltese feeding practices in yourself— you will better protect your pet's health and overall well-being.

Basic Nutrition

Next to breakfast cereals, supermarkets devote more shelf space to pet foods than to any other general category of products. In fact, research indicates that the pet food industry has grown mightily in the past two-and-a-half decades, and competition is tough between the leading pet food manufacturers for shelf space. Since 1974, dog food sales reached $3 billion and have maintained a steady upward trend ever since, with corresponding millions being spent each year on dog product advertising, from television to pet magazines to mainstream periodicals.

But despite what some of that advertising may claim, in terms of basic canine nutrition, one brand does not fit all. Proper canine nutrition depends on a number of factors, including the dog's size, her activity level, her age, and her

A Maltese's health and longevity rely on proper nutrition and healthy eating habits that start as soon as a puppy begins to eat solid food.

living conditions. You should also consider dogs with special nutritional needs, such as pregnant females, high-powered athletes, lactating moms, growing puppies, and dogs struggling with illness. Puppies, for instance, need more protein and carbohydrates in their diets, but as adults they should receive less protein to help prevent kidney problems.

Proper nutrition for all dogs is based on a balance of proteins, carbohydrates, fats, vitamins, and minerals. But that balance differs between a Maltese that spends a great deal of time in a person's lap and gets occasional exercise retrieving a ball or chasing the cat, and a Malamute that pulls a dogsled for a living. Age, health, and environment all play important roles in determining the ideal diet to meet your pet's nutritional needs.

Feeding a Small Dog

As a dog owner, you should understand that feeding requirements vary by life stages. These

═MALTESE MEMO═

Essential Nutrients

Every dog requires balanced rations of the following nutrients to maintain a healthy mind and body.

Proteins. Among other functions, high-quality proteins are required to build healthy bone, muscle, and blood.

Carbohydrates. Sorry, Dr. Atkins, but dogs need carbs for energy and proper brain function.

Fats. Another essential energy source, fats must be offered sparingly, preferably only as an ingredient in commercial dog food.

Vitamins and minerals. These are essential for almost every function of the body, but they must be balanced within the dog's diet. An excess of certain vitamins and minerals can cause severe health problems.

Water. Yes, water is a nutrient, so make sure your Maltese has plenty of the wet stuff—fresh and clean—available at all times.

---

hand, suggest excellent digestion. Regular elimination habits are also a sign that all is well in your pet's digestive tract. If you are feeding your pet properly, this will be reflected, as well, in a coat that is glossy, pliant, and clean looking.

As for the amount to feed your Maltese, adjust the volume so that your pet is neither fat nor too thin. Generally, a dog is overweight if you place both hands around her midsection and cannot feel ribs (unfortunately, a not-all-that-uncommon condition among pampered toys). Of course, your dog is too thin if your hands feel skin stretched over the ribcage. Seek a happy medium. A preferred weight for an adult Maltese is 4 to 6 pounds (1.8–2.7 kg), although some are a bit larger (bigger boned). Let your own pet's body type be your guide.

As for how to feed your Maltese, most adult dogs do well on two daily feedings—morning and evening—although twice-a-day feedings may not be compatible with your schedule. If you feed once a day, do it early to allow for optimum digestion and waste elimi-nation, followed by a healthy dog biscuit or two in the evening to take the edge off until breakfast. Make sure that your dog's food dishes are clean, and always keep a supply of fresh, clean water available.

When the Diet Changes

Remember, too, that changing a dog's food or water supply can have an adverse effect on the animal's digestive system. The canine diges-tive tract typically locks in to particular feeding times and foods, so maintain a consistent feed-ing schedule and food products to ensure your dog's digestive efficiency. Sudden changes can, literally, be a shock to your dog's system. To

are generally identified as *growth* (puppy), *maintenance* (adult), and *geriatric* (older). At about 8 to 10 months of age, the Maltese's total nutrient requirements gradually begin to decrease, so adjust your feeding regimen toward a healthy adult maintenance program.

The way you feed your dog is typically deter-mined by the dog herself. In order to under-stand this, you must observe her stools (fecal matter) on a regular basis. Excessively loose or foamy stools, pale stools, or stools the color of your dog's food indicate poor digestion. Smaller, darker, and firmer stools, on the other

*Bright eyes; a silky, flowing coat;
and high energy levels are signs
of a healthy, balanced diet.*

change a dog's diet—say, when the new puppy joins your family or an aging adult is switching to a food for older dogs—add a little of the new product to the old fare. In subsequent feedings, reduce the amount of the former food and increase the amount of the new food over time until you've made the complete transition.

Dogs don't usually object to a change in flavor as long as the basic diet remains the same, but they don't require constant changes in flavor either. A dog's eating habits are dictated primarily by her sense of smell. That is, it's okay to add a little chicken or beef broth to your dog's dinner from time to time for flavor variety, but don't necessarily count on flavor to whet your pet's appetite. The bottom line is this: A bowl of brand X that suddenly and totally replaces the usual brand Y will probably result in brand Z diarrhea.

Choices, Choices

In the last three decades, the pet food industry has experienced a revolution of sorts in consumer education and pet food research and knowledge. This has resulted in grocery and pet-supply store shelves loaded with high-quality commercial foods that meet standards almost as stringent as those for foods manufactured for humans. Entire lines of prescription diets are also available from veterinarians to combat such canine health concerns as heart disease, urinary tract disorders, and even dental problems.

With so many options, choosing the right food for your dog can be further complicated by the types of foods available. When you go dog food shopping, you will find canned foods, semi-moist foods, and dry foods. Or, if you are really brave and a have a lot of spare time on your hands, you can even try making your own.

Canned dog food is appealing to the olfactory senses of a dog, and it is usually used by veteran dog owners to flavor dry diets. About 50 percent of its protein content is from meat, fish, or poultry, and the remaining is derived from eggs, dried milk, and meat by-products. The average can of dog food contains carbohydrates of corn, barley, and/or wheat, as well as a combination of vitamins and minerals. Many owners of small dogs like the convenience of canned food, but it can be costly considering that you are paying for a water content of approximately 75 to 80 percent.

When you must change your Maltese's diet, replace the old food with the new a little at a time over the course of several days to avoid gastric upset.

manufacturers for each stage of a dog's chronological development, as well as various levels of activity and lifestyle. There are even canned dog foods for older dogs with kidney, heart, and other physical health disorders. Although they work well as flavoring agents, canned foods are not the best choice for the fostering of healthy teeth, and they can produce soft stools.

Semi-moist foods have about half the water content of canned foods. Because they come in individually wrapped packages, they require no refrigeration and are a convenient choice for travelers. The contents of a 6-ounce pouch or patty look like hamburger and contain about the same number of calories as a 1-pound can of dog food.

If, however, you have been feeding your dog canned or dry foods, be very cautious about the transition to a semi-moist diet. These foods not only fail to promote healthy teeth and optimal stool quality, many also contain unnecessary artificial coloring. Like canned foods, however, they can be a novel flavor enhancer for dry food.

Dry dog food usually comes as kibble, pellets, or flakes. Dry food is a combination of meat meals, grains, and vegetable products supplemented with minerals and vitamins that bring the product up to the standards outlined by the Association of American Feed Control Officials

At one time, canned dog and cat foods made up about 90 percent of all pet food sales. From a purely commercial standpoint, canned dog food may be the easiest for the new dog owner to use. It is offered by nearly all major pet food

Careful consideration should be given to choosing the proper food as there are many brands on the market.

The correct diet for one Maltese may not be ideal for another. Get to know your dog's specific dietary needs.

(AAFCO) and the Pet Foods Institute (PFI). If the food you choose does not state on its package that it meets these standards, find another food. Of the three types of commercial foods, dry foods are typically the least expensive choice. They come in boxes and bags as small as 2 pounds (0.9 kg), which can come in handy for keeping a small dog's food fresh.

Initially, the departure from canned dog food products to dry had a lot to do with convenience and storage. It was the same when canned goods became popular for people. It accelerated meal preparation, but it also created some domestic squabbles in households where the residents preferred fresh vegetables and meats to the canned varieties. Luckily, your little companion's appetite is not inhibited by such preferences. Whether you choose canned or dry, dogs will be stimulated by the smell and the taste of the gourmet delight you are offering. Although every meal on your dog's menu is the same, each one is a measure of your special attention.

High-quality dry dog food products are con-venient to use and store, they are good for digestion (evident in the small, firm stools they produce), and they help to keep teeth and gums healthy. Most professional "doggy" people recommend feed-ing dry foods. I have fed the same brand of dry dog food for more than 30 years with no known

There are three major forms of dog food—dry, canned, and semi-moist.

adverse effects, having been fortunate enough to find a product that has remained more or less consistent in quality.

Finally, we come to **home-cooked diets** for dogs. There are people out there who choose this option, but it cannot be pursued half-heartedly or ignorantly. A healthy homemade canine diet requires that an owner not only become educated about canine nutrition, but also have available the often specialized ingre-dients required to create a balanced canine meal. In my experience, most owners who start out with good intentions ultimately decide to leave the science and art of their pets' diets to the experts.

Once you decide what to feed your dog, that decision need not be set in stone. If you choose a food that seems to cause poor fecal quality or chronic gastric upset, your dog's system is try-ing to tell you that perhaps a

High quality dog foods are available in various forms (canned, dry, and semi-moist), as well as for specific life stages (puppy, high-performance, senior).

change—a gradual change, remember—is in order. Observe, as well, your dog's energy and activity levels and her general well-being. If your pet seems happy, robust, internally healthy, and active with a good appetite, and if her coat appears healthy and lustrous, this is the first indication that you have made a good feeding choice.

The Cost-Effective/ Health-Effective Diet

Quality improvements in nutrition have resulted in our dogs living longer, free of the health problems once caused by inferior ingredients thrown into pet foods because they couldn't be used for anything else. In the long run, better dog foods cut down on pet health-care expenses. It has also been found that with higher quality and more nutritious food, a dog may need to consume less of that food to maintain a healthy body and mind. Therefore, better quality dog

food may indeed cost more, but the health of your Maltese is more important. Just remember the old adage: You get what you pay for.

How you feed has everything to do with health maintenance, as well. Fortunately, feeding a smaller dog does not involve some of the concerns inherent in feeding large dogs, who gobble their food and are thus at risk of the life-threatening condition known as canine bloat. Still, it's not a bad idea to moisten a Maltese's dry food with a little warm water in the interest of better digestion. You can also stimulate the appetite from time to time by substituting chicken or beef broth for the warm water.

The amount you feed is also critical to overall health. You can monitor proper feeding by administering the ribcage test and also by weighing your dog periodically. Most Maltese are overweight if they exceed 7 pounds (3.2 kg); 4 to 6 pounds (1.8–2.7 kg) is preferred depending on body structure and adult size. Determine what is normal for your Maltese and let that be your guide.

Dos and Don'ts

No Maltese nutrition chapter would be complete without a discussion of the dangers of table scraps. Yes, I said "dangers." Unfortunately, far too many dog owners equate love of a dog with satisfying the dog's desire for "people food." This can result in a sad, unhealthy, and overweight Maltese. If you are one of those compelled to share your sumptuous fare with your pup, remember that a dog's

A healthy, high-quality commercial diet is best supplemented with daily exercise and lots of love, affection, and attention.

digestive system is not a human food-processing plant. Therefore, it won't function well over the long term on the same foods you eat.

If you habitually supplement a dog's diet with table scraps, you are not only preventing her from eating the proper amounts of regular, balanced dog food that she needs. You are also sending her a message that her eating habits are based on when, where, and what you eat. Some dogs devote an unusual amount of time and energy developing begging techniques that are difficult to ignore. Share occasional table tidbits with them, but don't do it on a regular basis—and *never* directly from the table. Better yet, when you just can't say no, give your pet quality dog biscuits instead.

Contrary to outdated opinion, dogs and bones are not necessarily compatible either. Delicate, splinter-prone poultry and fish bones spell disastrous consequences for dogs. Pork bones and most beef bones can also splinter, especially when they get dry, and thus cause the same obvious damage to a dog's throat and insides. Dogs have choked to death and died from internal bleeding caused by bone punctures and bones lodged in the throat.

While we are on the subject of potentially dangerous treats, please do not feed chocolate to your dog. Chocolate contains the compound theobromine, which is toxic to dogs. Some authorities also caution owners not to feed whole-kernel corn, raw eggs, fried foods, and dessert treats of any kind. Which leads us to another "don't" that is worth repeating again and again: Please don't overfeed your dog.

Make sure she receives her proper ration to keep her healthy and spry (and longer lived), and make sure she gets plenty of exercise, too.

Another common mistake that dog owners make is tampering with a balanced diet by adding extra fats to increase the palatability of the food. Since dogs digest fat before other nutrients, excess fats in the diet can contribute to imbalances. Oversupplementation of any kind, including with vitamins or mineral supplements, can create problems more complex and difficult to diagnose or treat than simple diet deficiencies.

Ensure that your dog is receiving the sound and balanced minimum daily nutritional requirements of proteins, carbohydrates, fats, vitamins, minerals, and water. Add to this clean feeding utensils and unlimited amounts of your knowledge, consistency, and love. Good health and a long life are almost guaranteed if you follow that recipe.

GROOMING YOUR MALTESE

Choose a Maltese as a pet and, sooner or later—well, sooner—you're going to be faced with taking care of that glorious Maltese coat. His hair is somewhat like human hair insofar as maintenance goes: washing, brushing, combing—with perhaps an occasional trim around the feet or eyes to keep them clean. If your Maltese is gently and positively introduced to grooming, you'll be in business.

Grooming Starts Early

The coat of the adult Maltese requires daily care if it is to remain mat-free and glossy. Puppies must be taught from a very early age to lie quietly on their sides and allow you to brush and comb their hair, fiddle with their ears, and play with their feet and tails. Be warned, however, that Maltese puppies can be surprisingly strong bodied and strong willed; politely allowing himself to be groomed does not come naturally to the healthy puppy. Practice laying your puppy on his back on your lap every day until he becomes comfortable in that

That lustrous Maltese coat is the result of daily attention, good health, and a sound and skilled grooming regimen.

position. Then you can start brushing. Soon you will be able to introduce the puppy to a grooming surface or table of a more comfortable and convenient height, or you may choose just to use the floor.

Brushing the Coat

The typical Maltese can and should learn to enjoy frequent brushings and complete grooming sessions. This is a people dog, happiest when engaged in any activity involving family members with whom he shares a special bond. How fortunate, then, that the Maltese coat requires regular attention, with brushing as the cornerstone of the grooming regimen.

While the care of the coat of the Maltese show dog's coat would command an entire

─MALTESE MEMO─

Grooming Tools

To groom a Maltese properly, you will need the following tools:

✔ Small pin brush with stainless steel teeth.
✔ Small, rubber-backed slicker brush.
✔ Six-inch, stainless steel comb with rounded teeth.
✔ Small, portable blow-dryer.
✔ Pair of scissors with rounded tips.
✔ One-pint plastic water spray bottle.
✔ Canine shampoo and coat conditioner.
✔ Small face or pocket comb.
✔ Orthodontic rubber bands for topknots.
✔ Pair of toenail clippers designed for small dogs.
✔ Teeth-cleaning supplies.

The first step in Maltese coat maintenance is daily brushing from head to toe and everywhere in between.

After dampening an adult's hair to reduce the chance of tearing it out, brush the hair in layers.

book of its own, Maltese pets engaged in an average amount of daily activity need to be brushed at least every other day. The longer you wait between brushings, the greater likelihood of mats and tangles developing, and the longer brushing will take to complete.

The coat can mat fairly easily, and mats can be difficult to eliminate, resulting in painful hair-pulling that will not endear you to your Maltese. Indeed, it is usually kindest to cut the mat out. Better yet, stick to the regular brushing schedule and prevent matting altogether.

If regular and frequent brushing is a burden on your schedule, you may simply choose to keep your Maltese's coat trimmed to puppy-length (about an inch all over). This will facilitate healthy hair and skin and serve to retain

When making the topknot, first brush the hair away from the dog's eyes.

Next, part the hair in the middle and firmly gather the hair on one side of the head.

that adorable puppy appearance throughout adulthood. Regular grooming still remains a must, however.

Brushing Training

Begin your dog's training in the brushing department by teaching him to lie on his side while you gently pet and talk to him. You can do this on the floor or on any other surface where both you and your pet are comfortable. When the dog becomes completely accustomed to this procedure, which may require as many as five or six practice sessions—and perhaps a treat or two—introduce the brush. I recommend starting with the legs and tail because these areas are a little less sensitive. Continue talking to the dog to reassure him, and again, remember that praise is an excellent training aid. Repeat the procedure with the comb. Gentle persuasion and continuous reassurance ensure success.

As the puppy matures, so does his coat, and required brushing time will increase proportionately with the increase in coat length and density. For best results, layer the coat. That is, part

the hair at the skin and, using the pin brush, brush only the section that is exposed. Part the hair again elsewhere, and repeat the procedure until you have brushed the entire coat.

Finally, fold the hair backwards and make a ½ inch (1.3 cm) loop. Secure the loop with a latex rubber band and use a bow to cover it over. Repeat with the other side.

Techniques to Master

Given the nature of the Maltese coat, a spray bottle filled with water comes in handy when brushing, especially in dry environments. If you spray a fine mist on the coat after parting it and just before brushing, the task is much easier. The tensile strength of the dampened coat is greater, preventing the hair from breaking or tearing.

When you are finished brushing the dog's main coat, have your pet stand facing you and brush the top of his head. Part the hair in the middle of his skull down to the tip of his nose. Now, firmly gather the hair on one side of the head and make a loop of about one-half inch, folding the hair backward, away from the eyes. Then, using a small latex rubber band, secure the fold to make a Maltese topknot. Repeat the procedure on the opposite side of the head, making the knot in approximately the same position as the knot on the other side. Now

As with all grooming practices, teach your Maltese to tolerate bathing from an early age.

brush and comb the hair on the chest, down the legs, and between the legs. Finish by brushing and combing the tail. Your Maltese is now ready for a bath (but do remove the top-knots for the bathing ritual).

Bathing Your Maltese

Most Maltese learn to love their baths if you employ some patience and regard their safety. Secure footing is a must, as are special precautions to protect the eyes. There are no-tears pet shampoos that will not irritate those big dark eyes begging you to "get this over with quickly." When first introducing your Maltese to bathing, remember, too, that a jet of water coming out of a faucet or spray nozzle can be frightening to a young puppy. Start puppies off by merely introducing them to the water. Sprays can come later.

A bathtub or utility/laundry-room sink with a nonskid surface (like a simple bath mat) both work quite well as tubs. For the procedure itself, I personally do *not* recommend filling the tub. I find little benefit in allowing your dog to stand in water that's bound to get dirty. Instead, once the dog is accustomed to water, wet him thoroughly. I use a shower hose attachment and turn on the water in a gentle spray. Remember to adjust the water tempera-ture ahead of time to a tepid (lukewarm) level.

Shampoo and Rinse

Once the dog is wet, apply a ring of shampoo around his neck and ear area, then lather. If the dog has fleas, this "chases" them rearward and

Make sure to rinse the dog thoroughly to avoid skin and coat problems.

keeps them away from the dog's face and eyes. Work in the shampoo and lather, moving toward the rear and applying more shampoo as needed. Pay particular attention to the tummy, the private parts, and the feet, working the lather between the pads. When the dog's body is thoroughly lathered, use a washcloth or small sponge to wet and wash his face.

The most important part of the bath is the rinsing. To avoid serious problems, never leave soap or soap residue on a dog's skin or coat. Two or more rinsings may be necessary to remove all the suds. Watch the rinse water carefully, and if it still runs cloudy, rinse again. Once you are certain that your Maltese is ready to dry, turn your head slightly to one side and prompt your dog to shake his body. With some dogs, this is automatic, but others need encouragement. I've found that if you lean close and blow a few quick puffs of your breath right at

Thorough rinsing and complete drying are the keys to a successful Maltese bath.

a his nose, your dog will shake, but be quick, or you could wind up wetter than your dog.

Professional groomers recommend that you apply a cream rinse or conditioner to the coat before you begin the drying process. This not only enhances the luxurious appearance and texture of the coat, but it also goes a long way toward reducing tangling and matting between baths and brushings. Apply the rinse generously and work it into the coat, allow a few minutes for it to set up, and then rinse it out.

Good Drying Is Key

At this point, I use my hands as a squeegee, moving them gently down the body and legs, squeezing excess water out. After you are confident that you have squeezed out most of the excess water, wrap the dog in a towel and soak up the remainder of the dripping moisture. Be thankful that your Maltese's small size makes this such a relatively quick and easy procedure.

You should comb and brush your Maltese thoroughly before and after his bath to prevent the coat from matting.

Now move your wet pet to a warm and comfortable drying area—again, one with secure footing. The healthiest Maltese coats I've seen are blow-dried. If you have a tabletop or stand-mounted hair dryer, allow the warm (not hot) air to blow on the coat as you brush, which accelerates the drying time. Just make sure the dog is amenable to the noise and the rush of air, and keep the dog warm until he is dry. Once he is, your grooming session is *almost* complete. Besides redoing the topknots, it's time to tend to the teeth, ears, and toenails.

Teeth Cleaning Made Easy

One grooming task often overlooked by many dog owners is the care of the teeth. However, teeth cleaning is as important to canine health as any other aspect of dog care. Ideally, you should clean your dog's teeth at least twice a week. Your veterinarian can rec-

Routine care of your dog's teeth will help ensure he keeps those teeth throughout his life.

Trim your Maltese's nails regularly (and carefully) to prevent them from growing too long and causing lameness and foot injury.

ommend a toothpaste made for dogs (avoid people products, which can upset a dog's stomach), or you can use a mixture of ¼ teaspoon of salt and ½ teaspoon of baking soda. Wrap a damp cloth around a finger, dip the moistened cloth in the toothpaste or homemade mixture, and apply it directly to the dog's teeth using gentle massaging strokes until all sides of the teeth are clean and bright. Pet supply stores usually carry pet toothbrushes as well as pastes if you prefer.

Though it may not be their favorite activity, all dogs can learn to accept this important part of their grooming routine. Teaching them to do so is essential, as is the feeding of dry kibble to keep teeth clean. Supplement this with professional cleanings by your veterinarian once or twice a year, and you will improve your dog's breath, as well as his chances of keeping his teeth throughout his lifetime.

ready to clip his nails, snip only the tip, just where the nail begins to curve. If you cut too much, the nail will bleed, so keep styptic powder or similar products to stop bleeding handy for such emergencies. Reward your pet profusely for

Toenail Care

A dog's toenails grow and begin to curve into clawlike appendages if not trimmed every six to eight weeks. This growth pattern can cause a great deal of discomfort and result in lameness problems later in life. Consequently, the toenails should be trimmed regularly, especially if your dog stays primarily indoors, walking on soft, carpeted floors that will not naturally wear down his toenails.

Teach your dog to cooperate with nail clipping from an early age by first teaching him to tolerate you touching his toes. When you are

Remember to clip the toenails at an angle. However, be careful you don't clip too low.

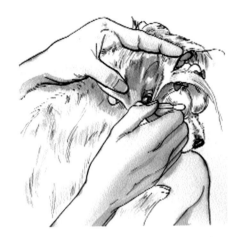

If you see dirt or wax buildup in the dog's ears, clean the ear gently with a moist cotton swab. Do not probe deep into the ear canal.

cooperating, and, if necessary, trim only a few nails per session. Your alternative, of course, is to have the job done professionally at a veterinary clinic or grooming salon.

Cleaning the Ears

Inside the Maltese ears, wax accumulates and fine hair grows. Throw a little dirt into the mix, and your dog could wind up with ear problems. Check the inside of the ears regularly. The interior sides of the ears should not only appear pink and clean, but they should smell clean as well.

If you spot a bit of dirt or wax buildup, clean the ear gently with a moistened cotton swab. I have a friend who recommends wetting the swab with a bit of mineral oil, but remember to mop up the residue with the dry end of the swab after cleaning. Don't attempt to clean the ears deep in the canal. Leave that for a compe-

tent veterinarian. Contact the veterinarian, too, if your dog starts shaking his head or pawing at his ears.

Maintaining a Clean, White Face

In between baths, pay attention to your Maltese's face to prevent skin or coat problems that can occur when the face hair gets untidy. For a clean, white face, comb the hair away from the eyes and mouth with your small, fine-toothed comb. Hair in the eyes causes tearing and possible staining of the undereye area. Medicated eye cleaners are available for cleaning in and around the eyes, and your veterinarian can recommend a safe product for your pet.

Once the staining begins, it is more difficult to get rid of than it is to prevent. Food and water can also affect hair staining around the mouth. Some people live in areas where the water has a high iron content, which can contribute to staining. Offer your dog bottled purified water or install a filter system to eliminate the problem. It's also wise to choose a food that is free of artificial colorings that will stain the white hair around your Maltese's mouth.

Some Maltese owners delegate the privilege of grooming to a professional groomer, and indeed, the entire process can be handled that way: brushing, bathing, teeth, toenails, and ears. Having your dog professionally groomed depends on your budget, and on locating a groomer who is not only gentle and skilled, but also experienced in caring for the unique Maltese coat. Whether you choose a professional or decide to go it alone, remember that a dog's cleanliness plays a major role in his overall health, happiness, and longevity.

Even if you opt to have your Maltese groomed professionally, you will still need to carry out the daily basics at home to ensure he remains the picture of health and beauty.

MALTESE TRAINING MADE EASY

Given the many parallels between successful dog training and child rearing, commonsense child-rearing strategies can actually come in handy when faced with the challenge of training a dog. Though you cannot expect human learning abilities from your dog, you can employ many of the same techniques that are used to raise children. You will also learn quickly that teaching a puppy is frequently a mutual learning experience.

Basic Training

Your Maltese's training should begin the minute she sets foot in your home. Establish the dog's boundaries quickly through strict scheduling and repetition, and bear in mind that a dog's entire recipe for contentment is founded on making her owner happy. Instinct guides her basic desires, and instinct tells her that life's rewards are derived from pleasing the "pack leader."

Repetition and reward are critical elements in any successful training program, whether you're teaching your dog basic good behavior

Training your Maltese from puppyhood through adulthood will help you both reap the rich rewards inherent in living with this lively breed.

skills, Dog Tricks 101, or advanced obedience. Dogs can be taught just about anything you have the patience and ability to teach. If your dog learns to walk on leash without pulling your arm out of the socket, and learns to obey the *sit, stay, come,* and *down* commands, she has fulfilled the basic requirements of being a well-mannered member of the family. You can teach these basics in six weeks or less depending on the frequency of your sessions and your consistency as a trainer.

Training Classes

Another option is enrolling your puppy in formal training classes. Most trainers prefer not to work with puppies under four months of age, but many offer puppy kindergarten classes for younger puppies. These classes employ training techniques geared toward the develop-

Whether enrolled in puppy kindergarten or upper-level obedience classes, the Maltese's intelligence, enthusiasm, and curiosity help to ensure her educational success.

ing minds and short attention spans of young puppies. A puppy kindergarten class with a very positive, puppy-loving trainer in charge is the ideal place for introducing your puppy to a lifetime of learning, as well as helping your new family member become properly socialized to a variety of people and other dogs.

From puppy kindergarten you can move on to more advanced classes that take advantage of an older puppy's expanding attention span. Training is an excellent investment in your puppy's life and in her future as a member of your family. If you decide to work with a professional, find a trainer who uses positive training methods, and who has experience working with tiny dogs. In other words, you want a trainer who will view the Maltese as a lively, intelligent student who wants more from life than simply living on your lap. Consult area experts for referrals: your veterinarian, a local kennel club, your dog's breeder, local groomers, and fellow dog owners.

Prepare Yourself

The operative words for your training regimen are *fun*, *common sense*, and *repetition*. You are the teacher. You are in control, but if you make it a contest, you'll risk losing the contest and possibly hurting your dog. Tolerance, understanding, repetition, and reward, as well as positive reinforcement, produce the greatest results, but at times there is a need for firm scolding. Achieving mutual understanding so that the dog understands what you are asking of her is the goal of training and will enable you to build your relationship on a firm foundation. You will achieve the ultimate reward of bonding and satisfaction when your dog responds to your commands and senses that she has pleased you. Sneak learning into your daily play sessions, but remember that even the smallest of dogs will get bossy if she thinks she is in control.

In training your dog, voice inflection and volume are very important. Some dogs are intimidated by loud voices but respond well to timid commands. Find the happy medium, and be enthusiastic with your praise for good responses. Offer treats only as an adjunct to verbal praise and your own body language. Allow your body to convey your pleasure with your dog's performance by clapping your hands, patting your pet's head, or scratching her behind the ears. On the other hand, turning away, averting your eyes, shaking your head, or even low growling can show disappointment and disfavor. From your own dramatic performances, your Maltese can learn when she has pleased you and when she hasn't.

Besides using food treats, some trainers whistle to get a dog's attention. If you don't whistle well, you can purchase a training whistle or a clicker at a pet supply store. The clicker attracts a student's attention or rewards the student for her obedience with its clicking sound. When you get to know your dog, you'll soon discover what pushes her all-important excitement and attention buttons.

First Steps First

The first and most important task in dog training is teaching your dog to walk on leash. In leash training, you are also teaching the dog to pay attention to you and to respond to your

Training not only makes your Maltese a better canine citizen, it also strengthens the bond between the dog and her family.

commands. All subsequent training is based on the dog's ability to be attentive and to respond.

To begin, you will need a metal-link slip-chain training collar, a 6-foot lead (nylon or leather, no chain) with a swivel snap, and your dog. We are speaking here, however, of a dog that is 6 months old or older. A younger puppy, whose neck muscles are not fully developed, should be walked only with a traditional buckle collar.

Most pet supply stores carry the leashes and training collars you need, and knowledgeable clerks can assist you in selecting the right size and style. To place the collar properly on your dog, hold one metal ring between the thumb

Are You a Dog-Show Prospect?

Just as you need to evaluate your dog as a potential show prospect, so must you evaluate yourself to see if you are up to this responsibility. Attending dog shows can be an exciting and rewarding experience if you:

1. Enjoy any activity that can be shared with a dog.

2. Enjoy competitive activities and the spirit of gamesmanship.

3. Function well in crowds and hectic atmospheres.

4. Like to travel and meet people who like to travel and meet people.

5. Have a flexible budget and infinite patience.

If you answered yes to most or all of these questions, then you just may be cut out for life as a dog-show devotee.

Always remember to give plenty of praise when your dog achieves a training goal.

and forefinger of your left hand with your other three fingers holding a portion of the chain, then grasp the other metal ring and extend the rest of the chain upward until there is no slack. Now, gradually, lower the raised end, allowing the slackening part of the chain to drop through the ring you are holding with your left hand so that a loop forms under the palm of your hand. Place the dog on your left side and face the same direction. Now slip the "noose" you've just formed over the dog's head, making sure that the ring you attach to the leash is at the end of the chain traveling over the top of the dog's neck from left to right. (See illustration in the HOW-TO section on page 66.)

Lead Training

After placing the collar on the dog, allow her to wear it for short periods of time for a few days to adjust to it. Monitor these sessions, and remember that the training collar must never be used as a dog's everyday collar. There's a very good reason why so many people refer to this as a choke collar, as it can easily be caught and tighten dangerously around the dog's neck.

When your puppy is ready, snap the lead onto the collar and let the dog drag it around for a little while to get used to it, too. Again, watch your pet to ensure she doesn't get the leash tangled on something and become frightened or injured. When you believe that your pet is somewhat comfortable with the arrangement, pick up the end of the leash and walk around with the dog, applying little or no pressure. Just follow your young student around. Gradually increase your control until the dog learns that even though the leash restrains, it is nothing to fear. When you reach

The better behaved and more reliable your Maltese, the more freedom she will enjoy beyond the confines of her home.

the point where you can persuade your puppy to come along in the general direction you have chosen, you are ready to begin the exercise that forms the foundation for all other training: heeling.

The Heel

For teaching the *heel* command, the slip-chain collar is designed to work as a "jerk and release" reminder or correction. The leash must always remain loose with *just enough* slack to allow you to give a short jerk to get your dog's attention during training. You must never, however, jerk the traditional buckle collar this way, as it can injure your dog's neck.

Once the collar and leash are in place, starting on your left foot, step out and say, *"Heel"* or *"Walk"* to your small student. You may pref-

ace the command with the dog's name to get her attention. Eventually, you'll be able to drop the verbal command altogether as the dog learns that when your left foot moves, it's time to go.

For the sake of training, let's call your dog Blanc (French for *white*). Holding the leash in your right hand, move your left foot forward, pat your left leg lightly, and say, *"Blanc, heel,"* or *"Blanc, walk."* Give a light jerk on the leash and be enthusiastic: *"Good dog, let's go!"* Walk in a straight line and each time your dog veers off or crosses over into your path, correct her direction with a quick tug on the leash in the opposite direction and continue walking. You're making progress if you can walk a dozen steps without needing to make a correction. Soon you can begin practice turns, always using the

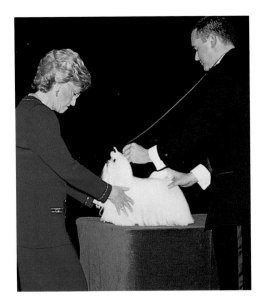

Show Maltese must learn not only how to "gait," alongside their handlers and tolerate intensive grooming, but also how to stand quietly while they are examined by judges.

master this skill, you are ready to tackle the other basic commands, the "how-tos" of which you will find at the end of this chapter.

Training for Show-Ring Success

There is much more to showing a Maltese than just making sure the dog sports a long, flowing coat. Grooming, breeding, and training all play critical roles in the process. Successful show dogs are carefully bred to meet the highest standards of structure, temperament, and health; religiously trained to conduct themselves properly in the show ring; meticulously groomed; and skillfully presented in the ring to the judges. If you are interested in showing, you will need to discuss your desire for a show-quality puppy with the breeder from whom you are considering buying your pet.

Each year, more than 10,000 competitive canine events are held under the auspices and guidance of the American Kennel Club. The most common of these are conformation showing and obedience trials.

To compete in the conformation show ring, a dog must be a purebred, it must be intact (meaning it has not been spayed or neutered), and it must be show-ring trained. Judges inspect and evaluate all parts of each dog from

leash as a guide and correction device—not as an instrument for tugging, dragging, or yanking on Blanc's delicate white neck. Your dog need not always heel when walking on leash, but she must learn not to pull on the leash. Once you

The ultimate endgame for the show Maltese is competing for Best-in-Show honors at the Westminster Dog Show in New York City.

If your aspirations include someday showing your Maltese, discuss this with the breeder, who may in turn be willing to match you with a potential show prospect and mentor you through the process.

nose to tail, so the dog must be trained to gait properly around the ring beside its handler, but also to tolerate the judges' hands-on attention. Looks and appearance are important, but so are temperament, the style of gait (or movement), the dog's overall condition and cleanliness, and how the dog is presented by the exhibitor.

Performance Events

While conformation showing is for those dogs who are the very best examples of their breed, virtually any purebred can be trained to compete in obedience trials, where attention is focused on dog-and-handler teamwork and performance. As smart and enthusiastic as they are, Maltese can do incredibly well in obedi-

ence trials, and they are very popular with spectators, who don't expect such beautiful little puffballs to perform so expertly. So don't underestimate your dog. The Maltese is certainly capable of acquiring the title of Obedience Champion.

Should you decide that showing of any kind is for you (and for your Maltese, of course), consider formal training for the canine activity of your choice. You might even be interested in joining a dog club, which can provide an excellent entrée into the world of dogs. Interaction with fellow club members can be the foundation for lifelong friendships, as well as a means of providing you with a solid education about this complex facet of dogdom.

Whether her training leads her to Best-in-Show honors in the show ring or success as a therapy dog, the Maltese's favorite role is that of family companion, which is equally reliant on a lifetime of training and consistency.

Practice, Practice, Practice

Let's say that your dog has been evaluated to be a promising conformation show prospect, and I've talked you into training and showing her yourself. What's the next step? There is a tremendous difference between wanting to show your dog and actually preparing the animal and yourself to take part in the glamour that is often found in "dogdom's square circle." The Maltese is a coated breed and just as much time is needed to get that coat ready for show as it is to get you and the dog prepared for showing it off.

Ideally, what you need now is an experienced exhibitor—perhaps your dog's breeder—who understands and respects your ambitions and who won't mind holding a novice's hand and walking you through the preparation paces. Attend a dog show and watch (in the grooming area) what a Maltese exhibitor goes through in preparation for the competition. Then watch how the dog is presented in the ring. Watch the dogs and their handlers carefully and try to determine if there are any significant differences. Each handler has a personally developed technique in presenting his or her dog according to its special characteristics.

The next step is to go home and apply what you have learned. Before you fill out your first pre-entry form for a dog show, however, there are at least three more elements to consider: practice, practice, and more practice. Whether you are aspiring to conformation ring greatness or some other canine activity such as agility or obedience, the more you practice, the more skillful you will become. No matter how great a specimen of the breed your dog is, and no matter how talented, faulty handling can have a negative influence on the judge's decision.

Other Avenues

In addition to conformation dog showing and obedience trials, there are other formal training venues in which you may want to participate with your Maltese, including agility trials and canine good citizenship tests.

Agility is a popular sport in which dogs, in partnership with their owners, traverse an

Maltese may be small, but they are just as enthusiastic as their larger cousins when it comes to such vigorous vocations as agility and obedience competitions.

obstacle course in an activity that promotes fun, exercise, and bonding. You can prepare for these events in agility training classes, and the events themselves are as exciting for the spectators as they are for the participants.

The American Kennel Club has also developed a program to encourage all owners to train their dogs properly. This program, the Canine Good Citizen Test (CGCT), emphasizes responsible dog ownership and proper canine behavior. Dogs of any age, purebred or mixed-breed, can take the ten-step CGCT, earn a certificate of accomplishment from the AKC, and add the title CGC to their names.

You might also consider training your Maltese to become a registered therapy dog. Therapy dogs visit elderly people in nursing homes, troubled children, or patients confined to hospitals, the animals' mere presence promoting human health and healing. You can find ther-

apy dog organizations in most areas that help prepare and train both owners and their dogs for patient visits.

Whether your Maltese has a show career, a calling for community service, or simply a life dedicated to pleasing her family makes no significant difference to the dog. The true measure of the quality of the human-dog relationship lies in mutual happiness and contentment. Dogs are the most versatile of companions. We share a relationship that dates back 30,000 years, and dog showing, obedience competition, and agility trials are only a small part of that association. More than anything, your Maltese is your faithful friend when you are in need of companionship, the unquestioning listener when you need to talk. If your Maltese is never formally entered in a dog show or other canine activity, she can still be the family champion running across your living room floor.

There are as many methods for teaching these basic commands as there are trainers, but I have found the following to be very effective with small dogs. Regardless of the method you choose—verbal praise, food treats, the clicker, etc.—make sure to praise your dog profusely and immediately; keep training sessions short; and never, ever lose your temper.

The Sit. *Sit* is a useful and easy-to-learn part of your Maltese's course of study. Holding the leash in your right hand about a foot from the slip-chain (you will probably have to bend over a little), lay your left hand on the dog's rump, exerting slight pressure downward while pulling up gently on the leash, saying *"Blanc, sit!"* If the response is positive, offer appropriate praise: *"Good dog! What a great dog!"* This command can also be taught by having the dog sit automatically when you stop walking after heeling at your left side. When you stop, give the command, *"Sit!"* Apply pressure with your hand on the dog's rump and after 10 or 15 seconds, give the *heel* command and begin walking, then *sit* again, and so on.

The Stay. Once your puppy has mastered the *sit* command, it's easy to teach *stay*. With your dog in the sitting position, give the command, *"Blanc, stay!"* Holding on to the end of the lead, back away

To teach the sit command, exert gentle pressure on your dog's rump while pulling up with equal gentleness on the leash and saying "sit."

from your dog. If Blanc follows, you say sharply, *"No!"* and reach down, pick up your dog, and put her down at approximately the same spot. Give the *sit* command and when she sits, praise her and give the *stay* command again. Back away slowly again and repeat the steps until you can back away to the extent of the leash length and stand. When Blanc stays for just a few seconds, return to her and praise her enthusiastically: *"Good dog! That's the way!"*

The Down. Teach the *down* command in the same fashion. After Blanc has mastered the *stay* command, from the sitting/staying position, give the command, *"Blanc, down!"* At the same time, place your left hand on the dog's rear

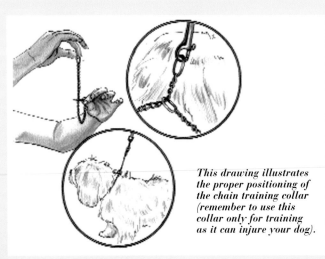

This drawing illustrates the proper positioning of the chain training collar (remember to use this collar only for training as it can injure your dog).

AND COME

end and gently grasp the lower part of her front legs with your right hand. Pull the front legs slowly and gently from under the sitting dog. This exercise may prove to be a test of your infinite patience. After Blanc is in the *down* position, give the *stay* command, and back away slowly. Repeat the steps from the beginning if Blanc gets up to follow, and issue that all-important praise if the attempt is successful.

The Come. Once *sit* and *down* are second-nature exercises, back away and issue the command, *"Blanc, come!"* If Blanc looks at you with a quizzical expression, you might say, *"It's okay, come,"* and as you say *"Come,"* give a gentle tug on the leash. Make sure your voice is as enthusiastic and as inviting as possible. You can try kneeling down at the end of the leash and patting the ground if Blanc doesn't come to you, but I'd be surprised if you have to do that more than once. Of all the tests to give a dog, *come* typically gets the most cooperation, because being close to you is the daily objective of your Maltese.

Nevertheless, I must offer a few cautions in the training of the *come* command to help ensure that you enjoy the greatest success possible. First, no matter how long it takes your dog to obey you, never correct or discipline her after she eventually obeys the command and comes to you. A scolding will confuse the dog, who will think, "I came and you scolded me!" She may not want to obey you again. In addition, a *lways* praise your dog when she responds to this command. And finally, when practicing the *come* command off-leash, do so only in a safe, confined area in case your dog chooses to run off rather than obey your command. (The same holds true for teaching *stay* off-leash.)

To teach the down command, place your dog in a sit position, then gently pull her front legs forward while pushing down gently on her rear end and saying "down."

Reward your small student every time she obeys the come command, even if it takes much time and effort for her finally to come to you.

THE CASE AGAINST BREEDING

Once you find yourself under the spell of an enchanting Maltese, you may realize that you cannot from that day forward live without one. And you would probably be right. You may also believe that you, and the world at large, just can't have too many of them. On that count, however, you would be wrong.

Too Many Dogs

The sad fact is that the world is filled with far too many dogs who do not have decent owners—or who do not have owners at all. As adorable and charming as the Maltese is, even this breed has fallen victim to the tragedy of pet overpopulation, and it is not unusual to find the black button eyes of one of these moppets looking out at prospective adopters from behind the bars of an animal-shelter cubicle. As unbelievable as this may sound, these puppies are given up every day both to shelters and to breed-rescue representatives. People move, children mistreat the tiny family pet, an allergy to dog hair emerges: The reasons for surrender are endless.

The question "to breed or not to breed" is critical to the well-being of the entire Maltese breed family.

Many of these so-called secondhand Maltese do ultimately end up in permanent, loving homes. But, sadly, not all of them do.

The message here is that, despite your many friends who may insist that they simply must have a puppy from your beloved Maltese companion (and that will happen, trust me), breeding is not something that most dog owners should contemplate, let alone pursue. You certainly don't want to add to the numbers of Maltese out there who may or may not be lucky enough to wind up in worthy homes. But pet overpopulation is only one reason not to breed your Maltese. A dog's health, behavior, longevity, and all-around quality of life are all intimately related to the breeding question. You must give a great deal of thought to these factors before you even imagine making your Maltese pet a parent.

Despite its many charms, even the adorable Maltese has fallen victim to the problem of pet overpopulation.

Making the Right Call

The decision to breed your Maltese or to have it surgically altered by spaying or neutering is difficult for some people—too many people, unfortunately. Carrying out the decision to alter a pet seems to be a threat to their own human sexuality, as dog owners are sometimes inclined to anthropomorphize their dogs.

Ideally the issue is taken care of by the breeder, who will insist that pet-quality puppies be spayed or neutered. It will surely be handled by the shelter or rescue group, rescuers being equally adamant about ensuring rescue pups are altered before entering their new homes. Nevertheless, there are still those who remain queasy at the thought of spaying and neutering. I hope to provide Maltese owners with some information that might help them make and carry out the decision to alter their companions.

Benefits and Consequences

In making the decision to spay or neuter, one cannot ignore the millions of healthy dogs being destroyed each year for want of responsible owners, or the profound health benefits of altering the family pet. The facts are clear. Time and time again, studies have shown, as have dogs themselves, that spayed and neutered pets live longer, live healthier, and are better companions. These facts alone should override any sense of fear or misguided anthropomorphic nausea that prevents owners from altering their pets. By taking a look at the details behind these facts, we should all feel much better about this important decision that all dog owners face.

Spaying

A normally healthy, intact female comes into heat every 6 months, and her cycle lasts for about 21 days. For most pet owners, this is a nuisance. The owner must contend with blood spotting and occasional surly moods from his or her darling little pet, not to mention the unwanted attentions of neighborhood males in pursuit of the resident female. Of course this can all be prevented by having the girl spayed, which will have far-reaching benefits.

Spaying is the surgical procedure that prevents canine pregnancy. It can be done anytime in a female dog's life, beginning at about 6 months of age (and in some instances even younger). Not only does spaying prevent any chance that your pet will find herself "with puppy," it will also reduce her chances of developing mammary tumors, uterine cancer, ovarian cancer, or life-threatening pregnancy and delivery complications. It is also believed that the younger a female dog is spayed—

Spaying and neutering are two of the kindest, most responsible procedures available to those who spend their lives with dogs.

ideally, before she experiences her first heat cycle—the better chance she has of avoiding these conditions later in life.

Neutering

Let's be honest. The male Maltese's role in reproduction is not what we might refer to as potentially life threatening. Unlike the female, whose job it is to carry and nurture the pups, the male does his job early on and he's done. But, believe it or not, there are profound health benefits to nipping in the bud the male's ability to play a role in Maltese reproduction.

Neutering, or castration, is a surgical procedure performed on male dogs, which includes the removal of both testicles. This, of course, prevents the male's ability to father puppies. In addition, altering a male is recommended to calm a male's aggression and to decrease his wanderlust should he decide to prowl the neighborhood in search of available females. It has also been very effective in reducing a dog's inclination to "mark territory," both inside and outside of the house. In addition to being an all-around calmer, more attentive companion, the neutered male may also enjoy better health and a better quality of life, thanks to the potential prevention of testicular cancer and prostatitis.

Dispelling the Myths

Despite the massive body of scientific evidence proving that spaying and neutering greatly enhance canine health and quality of

ᴍᴀʟᴛᴇꜱᴇ ᴍᴇᴍᴏ

Papers and Everything

Far too many people believe that a dog's purebred status—a status verified by those all-important American Kennel Club registration papers—somehow ensures that it will always be wanted, loved, and valued. Not so. Unwanted purebred dogs abound in our country—even unwanted Maltese. The Humane Society of the United States estimates that at least 25 percent of the dogs in animal shelters are purebreds. And, sadly, the breed rescue arm of the American Maltese Association is kept far too busy in its efforts to provide a safety net for unwanted Maltese throughout the country.

life, the myths connected with spaying and neutering continue to circulate. Even those myths that have for decades been exposed as false continue to be passed on from generation to generation. The sad result is far too many dogs being left intact and bred (either intentionally or by accident). Let's take a look at the big four.

Myth #1: Spayed and neutered dogs will become fat and lazy. **Fact:** Spaying can slow down a bitch's natural metabolism, the process that turns food into energy. Common sense would thus dictate that feeding your pup a fraction less food and increasing exercise and playtime would be the optimum way to counteract any effect spaying may have on a female Maltese's metabolism. Therefore, there is no reason for a spayed Maltese to gain weight.

The same holds true for the neutered male. Neutering will indeed reduce a dog's libido and metabolism; if you then provide a nice cushion for your Maltese male to lie on and feed him every time you eat without increasing his exercise, you'll wind up with a Maltese that can't get off that nice cushioned bed. The answer is simple: Feed responsibly and correctly, avoid excess treats, make sure your altered Maltese—male or female—gets plenty of exercise every day, and you will end up with a healthier pet with a longer potential lifespan.

Myth #2: Allowing a bitch to have a litter makes her a better pet. **Fact:** There is absolutely no clinical evidence available to support such a claim. In reality, just the opposite is true if you equate "better" with healthier and more even-tempered.

Veterinarians support the idea that spayed bitches experience far fewer serious health problems and make better pets. They also agree that puppies bred by novices with an average-quality dog are more prone to structural and genetic problems. And we would all probably rather not even think of the many puppies who find themselves in mediocre homes because their owners do not understand the rigorous screening processes that the best and most ethical breeders use to ensure the puppies they breed end up with the right people.

Myth #3: Surgery is dangerous and expensive. **Fact:** Modern advancements in both human and veterinary medicine have made surgery and anesthesia safer than ever before, even for young puppies. So avoiding spaying and neutering for the surgical-risk excuse really doesn't hold water. The same is true for the expense excuse. Acknowledging the many health and societal benefits of spaying and neutering, many veterinarians offer reduced rates for these surgical procedures, as do animal shelters and animal welfare organizations.

Myth #4: A female should be allowed to have at least one litter before she is spayed. **Fact:** There is no evidence that a female will benefit either physically or emotionally from having a litter of puppies. Some, in fact, can actually suffer physically from the experience, or prove not to enjoy the experience of motherhood.

Novices and so-called backyard breeders (pet owners who believe, perhaps, that their children should experience the miracle of life by witnessing the family pet have puppies, or those who would like to make a few bucks off that pet) may also be unaware of the risks involved when a small, perhaps even tiny, dog like the Maltese reproduces.

Pregnancy is a risk for any dog, so only that Maltese owner who is very experienced in selecting the perfect mate, seeing mom through the necessary prenatal care, and then helping with the actual delivery and follow-up care should make the potentially life-threatening decision to breed a Maltese. Having puppies does not make a female a better pet any more than fathering puppies makes a male a better companion. But spaying and neutering can indeed help to make dogs healthier, longer lived, and more relaxed and calm in the family circle with the people they love.

Contrary to the popular myths, a female Maltese need not have the experience of whelping a litter, and children need not experience the miracle of life by seeing the family pet go through what can be a potentially life-threatening ordeal.

The Cost of Breeding

Another reason to discourage the breeding of dogs is the high cost of doing it properly. Start with the veterinarian's fee for mom's prenatal health checkup and the tests required to ensure she is up to the task. Next, figure in the stud service fee for the male, which could range anywhere from $350 to $1,000. The price is usually determined by the stud's ancestry, his popularity, and his show career achievements. You might also try artificial insemination, but be aware that veterinarians charge a fee for this and for frozen sperm inseminations, and that does not include the cost of the semen.

Breeding can be potentially dangerous for tiny dogs like the Maltese, and it is not unusual for Maltese to have one-puppy litters.

with the American Kennel Club. A breeding investment could add up to $4,000 to $5,000, and with toy breeds, it is common to have one-puppy litters. That is a pretty expensive puppy, but nobody ever claimed that dog breeding was a profitable venture.

Final Considerations

If there is one reason not to alter a dog, it is the rule that dogs that have been surgically altered cannot be shown in dog shows sanctioned by the AKC. Yet the spaying and neutering of pets is a positive contribution toward reducing the numbers of abandoned and unwanted animals—even homeless Maltese—handled each year by animal shelters. If you have never undertaken the responsibility of animal breeding and birthing, leave it to the professionals.

I simply cannot overemphasize great cautions against—and the great dangers inherent in—breeding toy dogs. Whelping time frequently is accompanied by a cesarean section operation, which just as frequently results in the loss of the puppy, the mother dog, or both. In my mind, the loss of such a beloved member of the family is simply not worth the risk.

There is absolutely no point in breeding dogs unless there is a reasonable probability that you will produce better health, temperament, and appearance than that of your puppies' sire or dam. The only valid reason for breeding Maltese—or any purebred dog—is to *improve the breed.* The experienced breeder spends countless hours researching pedigrees to strive toward

Now add the prenatal care of the expectant mother, which may include the cost of ultrasound tests. Whelping doesn't cost anything unless you need veterinary intervention or a cesarean section operation (the latter is common with toy dogs). And you must not forget the cost of the whelping box and the other materials necessary for the delivery (towels, cleaning agents, and so on). Add the cost of the postnatal care of the dam to the equation, as well as that for the puppies' first medical health checks.

Before one puppy is sold, you could have a red-ink deficit of about $3,000, and the puppies haven't even had their first shots yet, nor have they been dewormed. Of course, you haven't figured in the time you've spent worrying, cleaning up after the puppies, and the trips back and forth to your veterinarian either. There is also the matter of registering the litter

The ultimate goal of Maltese fanciers, whether they be pet owners, breeders, and/or rescuers, is to see every Maltese in a permanent, loving home.

that goal, gaining the education and experience required to play matchmaker. If the primary purpose of every breeding is to improve the breed, secondary and subsequent reasons for breeding will take care of themselves.

There is also no point in breeding simply because everyone you know tells you they must have one of your puppies. Countless novice breeders have bred for this reason, only to find that once it is time for the puppies to move on to their promised new homes, they are no longer convenient additions to the prospective families. Then what do you do?

Even if you cannot be persuaded to alter your pet by the cost of breeding, the health risks of breeding, or the health benefits of spaying and neutering, keep in mind the most important argument for spaying and neutering. An altered dog is free to direct more attention toward his or her family rather than toward the cycles and scents of other dogs. The altered dog is more content to remain at home with the family rather than wandering the neighborhood in search of potential mates. In other words, altered pets make better pets! And that is a powerful argument indeed.

THE HEALTHY MALTESE

For the most part, Maltese are healthy little dogs, and that robust health should shine clearly from their beautiful black eyes. But maintaining that health doesn't happen automatically. The gift of health is one of the greatest gifts you can offer your pet, but only if you educate yourself about canine health and preventive action; learn what is normal—and abnormal—for your particular pet; and establish a relationship with a good veterinarian.

You and the Family Veterinarian

The health-care package that you obtain when you acquire the services of a good veterinarian is the very best form of medical insurance you can get. The same holds true for a trusted physician. Think of the times you have been sick or injured and how much better you felt immediately upon seeing a familiar face with a stethoscope. That trust and confidence are just as important to your dog as they should be to you.

The internal health of the Maltese is evident in such external indicators as the coat, the skin, the eyes, and the overall countenance of the dog.

Your veterinarian is your dog's second best friend. As your dog's *first* best friend, it's up to you to be the initial diagnostician when your little companion isn't feeling well. It's you who should be able to spot the trouble signs— changes in behavior, eating habits, activity levels, the color and character of his eyes, and the normal condition of his coat and skin—that could indicate a budding illness.

You thus play an important role in your pet's health-care game plan; the first and best line of care for your Maltese is prevention and detection. Your role as a Maltese owner includes both the daily maintenance of good health and clear communication with your pet's veterinarian. It is your job to become familiar with your dog's normal physical and emotional characteristics. If even a minor

⎯MALTESE MEMO⎯

Puppy Shots

The vaccines listed below are recommended for puppies and dogs that will be traveling, boarded, trained, or participating in activities that will bring them into contact with other dogs.

- Distemper
- Parvovirus
- Hepatitis
- Leptospirosis
- Parainfluenza
- Coronavirus
- Rabies (in most areas mandated by public health law)
- Lyme disease (optional)
- Canine tracheobronchitis (formerly "kennel cough")

Choose a veterinarian for your Maltese as soon as possible. If your choice is experienced with toy dogs, that's a bonus.

change is drastic or prolonged, contact your veterinarian. In most cases, early intervention promotes a quicker return to health.

Finding the Right Veterinarian

It may take you a while to find a veterinarian with whom you are comfortable, as the bedside manner of one practitioner may mesh better with some owners than with others. Nutrition and health care for dogs are as varied as the dog population itself, and veterinarians certainly should not view the needs of a Maltese in exactly the same way that they tend to the needs of a Great Dane or a working hunting dog. If your veterinarian does, then perhaps it's time to find a new veterinarian.

Keep in mind, too, that veterinarians don't really need sick dogs to sustain their practices. They have their hands full administering preventive medicine and attending to emergency situations. One of my dogs lived to be 17 years old. After he had his dewclaws removed as a 2-day-old puppy, he saw our veterinarian twice a year for physical checkups, teeth cleaning, and booster shots. If you stop to think about it, a veterinary clinic could stay very busy if, in addition to the occasional broken leg and unexpected trauma, every pet owner in a 10- to-15-mile radius of the clinic visited twice a year during each pet's lifetime for nothing but preventive care.

Immunizations

Routine immunizations play another important role in your dog's preventive health program. Today, vaccinations and annual boosters are slowly eradicating many of the common and potentially life-threatening infectious

The savvy Maltese owner knows what is and isn't normal for his or her dog, and is thus able to report potential problems to the veterinarian as soon as possible.

diseases that can afflict your pet. Back in the 1950s, rabies and distemper shots were sufficient, but now, a trip to the veterinarian for an annual booster shot will provide immunity for a variety of canine illnesses (see box, page 78).

Your dog should receive a series of puppy shots at regular intervals at 6, 8, 12, and 16 weeks of age. After that, one annual booster for everything is recommended (except perhaps for rabies, which may be required only once every three years). You may also choose to vaccinate your dog for such diseases as Lyme disease if you will be in an area where this tick-borne illness is common, or for tracheobronchitis (formerly known as "kennel cough"), a vaccine typically required of dogs in boarding kennels.

Signs of Illness

Knowing your pet as you do, it is your responsibility to observe and evaluate him daily for any small sign that could mean his health is at risk. As any physician or veterinarian will tell you, the earlier most illnesses are detected, the more easily and successfully they can be treated.

If your Maltese is frisky and fetching the ball one day, and the next day refuses food, is lethargic, and won't leave his pillow for his favorite game, you know instantly that something is wrong. Even everyday signs can alert you to trouble, so check your pet's fecal matter and urine daily for a change in color, consistency, or composition, and observe how much, or how little, food and water your dog is con-

suming. These, too, can indicate a budding problem, or even a serious emergency.

What it takes to keep a dog healthy is an owner who is willing to devote the necessary time and energy, not only to exercise, training, and grooming, but also to the observation and evaluation of the dog's activity level and state of mind. Conscientious care and preventive health measures are by far easier to administer and less expensive than treatments for life-threatening health conditions. If you notice any suspicious signs, such as blood in your dog's feces or urine, sudden weight gain or loss, coughing, watery eyes, lameness, a bloated abdomen, shivering or restlessness, obvious pain, an inability to defecate or urinate, persistent diarrhea or vomiting, or a deterioration of skin or coat quality, contact your veterinarian right away. You might just save your pet's life.

Now that we know the signs to look for in a potentially ailing dog, let's take a look at some of the problems that can plague our Maltese.

Skin Problems

The single most common and irritating problem affecting our dogs is skin irritation. Classic signs of dermatological problems include itching, scabs, redness, sore and moist patches of skin, swelling, hair loss, dandruff, scaling of the skin, discoloration, lumps and bumps, and purulent discharges.

Allergies. Some of the above skin problems can be caused by allergies. Pollen, dust, molds, insect bites, flea medications, and certain foods can launch allergic reactions in a dog. The first, best action to take when any of the aforementioned signs appear is to contact your veterinarian to help you isolate the cause and figure out a successful treatment plan.

Seborrhea. Another skin problem that affects dogs is flaky, scaly seborrheic skin. In extreme cases, this condition may be incurable, but in all cases, diagnosis and treatment should be left up to your veterinarian. Like all canine skin problems, it is a condition that is greatly aggravated by itching and scratching, which some dogs will do to the point of mutilation.

Hot spots. This is a common problem among heavier-coated dogs. Hot spots appear as round splotches of painful, moist, and swollen skin, and they must be treated by your veterinarian. Hot spots can be caused by, among other things, an improper diet, fleas, impacted anal glands, a dirty coat and skin.

External Parasites

External parasites like fleas, ticks, and mites can be the cause of great skin discomfort for your dog. Anyone who has ever watched a dog scratch incessantly at tiny specks scampering around his ears or belly can testify to that. But these parasitic monsters don't stop there. If given the chance by dog owners who ignore them, their infestations can lead to the development of far more serious health problems for host dogs.

Flea Treatment and Prevention

The most detestable of the dog's parasitic pests is, of course, the flea, the ageless adversary of dogs and dog owners. In the war

A Maltese who suddenly loses his appetite or his interest in play is a Maltese who isn't feeling well and should be examined by his veterinarian. Remember, too, that early detection often means more effective, less traumatic, and less expensive treatment.

against fleas, you attack the fleas on the dog, you attack the fleas in the home and where your dog sleeps, and you attack the fleas where your dog plays and eliminates waste.

Every eight to ten days, in ideal flea-friendly conditions, the hardy flea egg becomes a new larva that quickly evolves and begins reproducing its own population of blood-sucking adult fleas. Fleas eat by siphoning blood from their host and then reproducing at that rapid rate. The female flea lays eggs on the host, in bedding, in carpets, and on the ground. The eggs laid on the host dog do not necessarily cling to the skin and coat; they can fall anywhere the dog roams.

Commercial products available for flea control have traditionally included flea collars, shampoos, sprays, powders, and dips, their major drawback being the fact that their effects were often temporary. Today, however, newer, longer-lasting products, including oral and systemic spot-on insecticides, have been developed. As one might expect, flea control can be somewhat expensive and frustrating, especially in warmer areas where flea infestations are common year-round. The good news is that with the newer oral and topical systemic treatments and products on the market, flea control is becoming much safer, more effective, and more environmentally friendly than it used to be.

One group of these products, called insect growth regulators (IGRs), works to interrupt the development of fleas by killing flea larvae and eggs. These products do not kill adult fleas, but they dramatically decrease the flea population by arresting the development of fleas in

Recent advancements in flea prevention have greatly reduced the suffering of dogs at the jaws of these irritating little parasites.

premature stages. Depending on the particular product, an IGR may be given orally on a monthly basis (and may be combined with a heartworm preventive to tackle both parasites simultaneously), or administered by injection every six months. Other effective forms are available as sprays or collars.

Another family of products, adulticides, kills the actual flea and works quite rapidly. These include both spot-on and oral products. Spot-on products are usually applied to your dog's skin in the area between the shoulders. The medication is absorbed into the skin and distributed throughout the body, killing the fleas rapidly when they make contact with the skin.

For most dogs, these products are safe, easy to use, and effective. As we have seen, some have the added benefit of efficiently targeting other parasites as well. Some veterinarians even recommend a combination of an adulticide and an IGR as a more complete method of flea control.

With all these choices, it is best to consult your veterinarian about the best program for

═MALTESE MEMO═

Scabies Alert!

It is important to remember that scabies can affect a dog's owner as well as the dog. Indeed, scabies is one of the few diseases that are transferable from canine to human. If you suspect you may be sharing your pet's infestation, get to the doctor right away. As with your pet, the earlier you start treatment, the better your chances of victory.

Consult your veterinarian about products to use in the fight against external parasites. What is safe for adult dogs, for example, may be dangerous for young puppies.

your pet, as not every dog can tolerate every form of flea control. The choice of flea control should depend on your pet's lifestyle and his potential for exposure, as well as his own health and condition, which may make some products safer choices than others.

Fleas at Home and on the Dog

Through the faithful use of systemic monthly flea products, the total flea burden on your pet and in your family's immediate environment may be dramatically reduced. Keeping your pet on monthly flea treatments, especially in areas of high flea risk, is an excellent preventive method, and you may find that these products greatly reduce the need for routine home insecticidal use. In most cases, however, it remains prudent, especially in heavily flea-infested environments, to treat the premises as well.

The first step in any three-pronged flea-control program, whether or not it is combined with the new oral and topical remedies, is to choose high-quality products. First, bathe your dog using a high-quality flea shampoo. Again,

your veterinarian or your dog's groomer can recommend a good shampoo for your Maltese's particular needs. Follow the instructions carefully. After the bath, rinse your dog thoroughly, then take him somewhere away from the house for a few hours. Before you leave, set off pesticide bombs, again following the directions on the label, and shut the house up tight.

Ideally, you should also wash your dog's bedding, treat your car interior with a safe flea-killing agent, and spray the yard with a flea-killing pesticide. When you return to the house, air it out, vacuum everything thoroughly, and dispose of the vacuum cleaner bag.

Then congratulate yourself. You have, for the time being at any rate, won the first battle of the ongoing war against the mighty flea.

Ticks

Ticks can cause anemia (a lack of iron in the blood) and such diseases as Lyme disease and tick paralysis. If you live in an area where ticks reside, check your dog's skin and coat regularly, and remove any ticks as soon as you discover them. The easiest way to remove a tick is to grasp the entire tick with tweezers and firmly, though gracefully, pull it straight out.

Once the tick is gone, disinfect the site thoroughly, and stay alert for the next few days for classic signs of illness. In this case that means an overall weakness, joint pain, unexplained

fatigue—anything out of the ordinary, as these can be a sign of tick-borne illness.

Mites

There are different kinds of mites that cause the problem generally known as mange. Two of the more common mange mites are *Demodex canis* and *Sarcoptes scabei*. The initial signs of demodectic mange are small patches of hair loss around the forehead, eyes, muzzle, and forepaws. Medicated dips are usually effective in destroying the mites, but dogs with generalized demodectic mange should not be used for breeding.

Scabies, on the other hand, is characterized by intense itching and hair loss, especially in the areas around a dog's ears, legs, and face. If allowed to go untreated, your pet's entire body could become affected. Once your veterinarian has determined that your dog has scabies, the animal will require several treatments with insecticides and, possibly, antibiotics and steroids to help relieve the itching until the mites are destroyed.

Ear mites, or *Otodectes cynotis,* live and feed in your dog's ear canals. Infected dogs shake their heads and scratch at their ears incessantly. You may also notice a dark-colored waxy substance inside the ears, which may be accompanied by a strong odor. Your veterinarian can teach you how to keep your Maltese's floppy ears clean and avoid ear mites, and only he or she can help you get rid of them should your dog become an unfortunate victim.

Both internal and external parasites lay in wait throughout your dog's environment. You must thus stay on the lookout for signs of infestation all year-round.

Canine parasite infestations are unpleasant and debilitating to your dog's overall health, but for the most part they can be successfully controlled if recognized soon enough. Never allow suspicious conditions to go untreated, and avoid the impulse to forego professional treatment in favor of questionable home remedies or cheap over-the-counter concoctions. When in doubt, contact your veterinarian. And do it early!

Internal Parasites

Internal parasites are more commonly known as worms, and there are all sorts of misconceptions, myths, and misinformation about them. Have you ever heard, for example, that dogs who eat candy and other sweet confections will get worms? I guess that if the candy was infested with worms, your dog could ingest the larvae and become sick with worms, but that's not likely.

Technically referred to as endoparasites, internal parasites tend to make their homes in a dog's intestines and other internal organs. They can cause chronic disorders of these organs, resulting in a variety of biological and physical behavior changes in the host dog—and sometimes even death. The most common internal parasites are roundworms, hookworms, tapeworms, whipworms, and heartworms, as well as single-celled parasites, such as coccidia and giardia.

If you follow a program of twice-a-year health check-ups for your dog and learn to observe changes in your dog's behavior, feces, and overall condition, you can prevent 90 percent of potential internal parasite problems. You can eliminate the other 10 percent by

═MALTESE MEMO═

Advice on Medicating

I strongly recommend that every pet owner consult a veterinarian before giving a pet oral medication or applying any topical medication. I also caution you against using a medication that another pet owner has used and given to you for a pet that you assume is experiencing a similar problem. Never use a medication on your dog that was previously prescribed for another dog. Finally, over-the-counter medications can cause your dog more problems than the ailment you are trying to treat without veterinary advice. So get that veterinary advice first—and follow it.

observing proper sanitation protocols and monitoring what your dog ingests.

Roundworms

Scientifically called *Toxocara canis*, these are large worms that reach 4 to 8 inches (11–21 cm) in length. As egg-laying adults, they live in the small intestines of dogs younger than 6 months of age. Approximately 75 percent of the puppies in the United States are infected with this parasite, which passes its eggs in its host dog's feces.

Heavily burdened puppies appear potbellied with dull, dry coats. They will occasionally pass entire worms in their stools or even vomit them. Roundworms look like cooked spaghetti. Their eggs are transferred to unborn or nursing pups from a mother dog, in whose muscular system they reside quietly. It is from here that

Though the Maltese may qualify as a classic housepet, he thrives both physically and emotionally on daily activity in the great outdoors with his human family.

they launch their attack, penetrating through the placenta and making their way into the mother's milk. Puppies can be safely treated for roundworms as early as 2 weeks of age. From then on, take a fecal sample to your veterinarian every time your dog has a check-up, just to make sure that worms of any kind have not made your pet their host.

Hookworms

Hookworms are not as prevalent as roundworms, but in some southern states, the hookworm problem has been quite serious. While hookworms cannot penetrate the placenta, they can enter the milk of nursing bitches. Hence, pups can become infected early in life.

Hookworms, named for the "hooks" inside their mouths that can cut through an intestinal wall, move from site to site, leaving a trail of bloody splotches behind them. Consequently, infected dogs often present bloody stools and suffer from anemia. Heavily infected puppies can die if the anemia is severe enough. All dogs may contract hookworms by swallowing the parasitic larvae, or the larvae can penetrate the dog's skin. Debilitated dogs are easy targets, and heavy infestation can cause death.

A hookworm infestation is treated the same as an infestation of roundworms. Treat the environment, as well, with 10 pounds of sodium borate per 100 square feet. Hookworms are also a health threat to children, so keep toddlers away from all puppy fecal matter. As prevention, keep your lawn cut short and wash down paved areas with disinfectants.

Whipworms

Whipworms, *Trichuris vulpis,* are also characterized by fecal/oral tramsission. That is, the larva is passed from an infected dog to another dog when the uninfected animal comes in oral contact with infected feces. When this occurs, whipworms take up residence in the lower digestive tract of the host dog.

These worms are shaped like a whip, hence their name. They thread their narrow end into the lining of the colon to hold on and lay their football-shaped eggs. Whipworm eggs are virtually indestructible, and once your yard is infected, it basically remains so. The big problem is that classic signs of whipworm do not appear in all dogs, but most will display mucus and blood in their stools. Some dogs even vomit due to a phenomenon called colonogastric reflex.

Tapeworms

Tapeworms, or *Dipylidium caninum,* survive by way of a complicated indirect life cycle, which mandates that they pass through two hosts: a dog and a flea. To treat a dog effectively for tapeworms, then, the flea problem must also be eliminated. (See previous sections on flea control.)

Tapeworms may be noticed in the hair around a dog's anus, in the dog's bedding, or in the stool itself. Tapeworm segments are off-white and look like grains of rice. If your dog is eating well but losing weight, has occasional diarrhea, and is lethargic, look for the rice-like segments clinging to the fur around his rear end. If you find them (and even if you don't),

contact your veterinarian. He or she is the only one qualified to combat this parasite.

Heartworms

Heartworms are nematodes that live within the chambers of the heart. Following the bite of an infected mosquito, young heartworms enter the bloodstream of the dog and actually mature within the canine heart, where they may reach a length of 5 to 12 inches (31–31 cm). Needless to say, heartworms present a serious, life-threatening problem to infected dogs, who typically tire easily, cough chronically, and lose weight.

Dogs already infected with heartworms may be treated with drugs to destroy the worms, but preventive medicine before the fact is a better option, as treatment can be just as dangerous to the patient as the infestation itself. Try to control the mosquito population in your dog's environment, and give your pet heartworm preventive medications, which are available from your veterinarian. The doctor will want to examine your dog and take a blood sample before you begin this program, but it is worth the effort and expense to get such a program underway for your pet. Just ask anyone who has ever nursed a dog through heartworm treatment—or lost a dog to this parasite.

Coccidia

Coccidia are single-celled organisms that can inhabit the intestinal tract of dogs. Infections are most commonly seen in young dogs and puppies. Filth and overcrowding are thought to perpetuate the disease. Coccidia infection is usually accompanied by bloody diarrhea.

Treatment is difficult because only a few sulfa-type antibiotics are effective. If medication is not administered for an appropriate period of time (some veterinarians treat their patients for 21 consecutive days), recurrence is common. As with whipworms, coccidia seem to infest surrounding property as well as resident dogs, so regular disinfectant cleaning and the replacement of whelping boxes are recommended.

Giardia

Giardia is another single-celled organism that infects the digestive system of dogs. Many water supplies and lakes are reservoirs for *giardia,* so it can be a serious threat to dogs who enjoy hiking in the great outdoors with their caretakers (and a threat to those caretakers, too). Signs of infection may be vague, though intermittent diarrhea is a common symptom. Here, too, it is wisest to consult your dog's veterinarian (as well as your physician) for treatment.

Exercise, Exercise

We really can't make our way through a chapter on Maltese health—or the health of any breed—without touching on the subject of exercise. Yes, the Maltese is a toy dog, but it is still a dog, and all dogs need exercise if they are going to reap the wonderful benefits of long-term health and well-being.

You might think that owners choose a Maltese simply so they can install the pampered pet on the sofa, feed him bonbons and ice cream, and sit back and gaze upon his beauty. Do that, and your little white friend won't be around for long. Besides, Maltese are fun-loving, adventurous little creatures. They want and need activity, though of course not as much or as intensive as, say, an Iditarod sled dog. Many a Maltese enjoys formal activities, such as obedi-

ence training and competition, but your exercise program need not be excessive. Keep it simple and make it part of the daily routine. I would venture to say there isn't a Maltese among us who doesn't love a daily walk with his owner or his entire family. You'll notice this when you see him jump with joy as soon as you just look over at the leash hanging by the door.

The Time to Say Good-Bye

The very worst part of having a dog in your life is the fact that, relatively speaking, a single dog is not in your life for very long. Maltese are ancient at 15 years of age, and the day will come all too soon when you have to say goodbye. One of the most difficult responsibilities of dog ownership is making the decision to end the life of an old friend, and most of us who have lived with dogs have had to do this at one time or another.

When faced with this decision, ask yourself the following questions: Is life still fun for your dog? Can your dog get up and down without pain, move without discomfort, eat heartily, and eliminate waste without a problem? Sometimes all a dog has left is his dignity, and he trusts us to ensure that his dignity remains intact. If your dog cannot exist within the dignified boundaries where he has lived all his life as a member of your family, then life probably isn't much fun or even pleasant anymore. You must then do what is decent and end his suffering. This is the time when you and your veterinarian should discuss the humane act of euthanasia.

When you make this courageous decision, spend time remembering the happy times you have spent with your beautiful little friend and

The joy of living with a Maltese far surpasses the pain of loss when it is time to say good-bye to one of these beautiful little characters.

all the fun activities you shared. Try not to dwell on the loss, but instead glorify the relationship and all this little dog has contributed to your life. Dig out the old photographs and recall the funny antics, the cute habits, and the brilliant tricks that made your Maltese so very special.

Once your pet is gone, give yourself some time to heal and to grieve, but don't deny yourself happiness based on the possibility of future pain. We've all heard people claim, in the wake of a beloved pet's death, that there will be no more dogs in the household. It's just too painful when they must leave. Remember, too, that when you do take the plunge again, no dog can ever take the place of the dog you just lost, and it's not fair to expect that of a new dog who enters your household. It would be a study in frustration to find a duplicate of your former companion, yet a new dog will generate its own special memories and find a little vacant spot in your heart, right next to the spot occupied by the dog who came and was loved before.

I once wrote these verses for a friend who had just lost a beloved Maltese:

Oh dog of white and silken hair, whose kennel bed now stark and bare;
You've left us the sun to light the dark and memories of your happy bark.
You've taught us love and loving cares.
You've left our cheeks with loving tears.
You've left our hearts with joyous years.
Rest now, our friend.

Maltese grow accustomed very quickly to spending quality time with their owners—all the time. Indeed, it is very difficult to leave them behind when you are pursuing new adventure yourself. As a result, Maltese can be prone to health threats that leave them in need of first aid while you scramble for veterinary assistance. Below is a brief introduction to some of the more common conditions that may require you to act quickly and possibly save your pet's life.

Bleeding wounds. While bleeding is the body's natural way of cleansing a wound, there is a big difference between a small, superficial cut and a bleeding wound.

The latter requires your immediate attention, as you may need to get the bleeding under control before taking the dog to the veterinarian.

First, cover the wound with a clean cloth, towel, or gauze. Apply direct pressure with your fingers, which may be all that is required to get the bleeding under control. Remove the material every 30 seconds to check if the flow has stopped. If it doesn't stop, or if it spurts rather than flows (the sign of an arterial wound), wrap more layers of material firmly around the wound and get the dog to the veterinarian immediately.

Shock. Shock is the body's response to such serious health conditions as broken bones or massive blood loss. Here, too, it is your job to keep the dog's condition under control so that you can get him to the veterinarian for treatment.

If, following a trauma, the dog is lying quietly with a weak but rapid pulse, shallow breathing, a low body temperature, and pale gums, death could be imminent if you don't act quickly. Keep the dog calm and comfortable, and place a blanket over him to keep him warm. Get any bleeding under control, and then get the dog to the veterinarian as soon as possible without moving him too dramatically, especially if you suspect broken bones or internal injuries. This task is much easier with a small Maltese, of course, than with one of his larger cousins. In most cases of shock, only a veterinarian is qualified to administer the treatment necessary to reverse the condition.

Choking. Maltese are curious little critters, and it is not unusual for one to find an interesting item on the floor and check it out with his mouth, only to have it lodge in his throat and block his airway. If you notice your dog

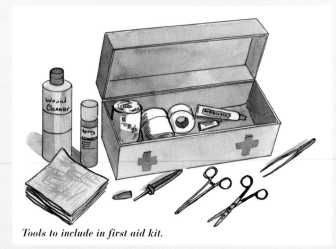

Tools to include in first aid kit.

opening his mouth as if to vomit, salivating, and/or pawing at his mouth with his paws, he is probably choking.

If the dog is still breathing, get him to the veterinarian immediately. If, however, he stops breathing and loses consciousness, pry his jaws open with the back of a screwdriver or similar object and try to see the offending object. You may be able to remove the object with needlenose pliers or tweezers. There is also a canine version of the Heimlich maneuver, but you will need to go over this with your veterinarian to ensure you know how to do it safely with such a small dog—*before* you ever have need to use it.

Poisoning. Again, curiosity has killed as many dogs as cats, so keep the number of your local poison control center posted prominently in your home should you suspect poisoning. There are as many remedies for poisoning as there are types of poison. If you suspect poisoning, try to find out what your dog may have ingested so you can tell the veterinarian or poison-control official in the event of an emergency. Wiser still is the owner who takes action to prevent poisoning, such as keeping pesticides and other poisons away from a curious Maltese, and making sure the family pet never has access to such sweet-smelling, sweet-tasting poisons as antifreeze.

Heatstroke. Maltese owners find it very difficult to leave their precious pets behind—even if that means leaving the dog in a car on a warm day. Even if the weather isn't hot, the

Garden chemicals are dangerous for dogs.

result can be heatstroke, a condition that can turn fatal very quickly.

If you notice your Maltese panting excessively and perhaps panicking and having trouble standing, you need to get him cooled down gradually. Remove the dog from direct sunlight (preferably into an air-conditioned house) and then immerse your pet in a tub of cool (not cold) water. Encourage him to drink small rations of cool water, and, as with any emergency, get him to the veterinarian right away.

Heatstroke is, of course, another emergency that can be prevented. Leave your Maltese home on warmer days (and remember that a mild temperature in a car can heat up to scalding in minutes). Even an open window or two may not sufficiently cool the car, and it leaves your dog at risk of being stolen. Take your walks and jogs with your pet during the cooler times of the day, and make sure that all day, every day he has access to fresh water and an escape from direct heat and sunlight.

Organizations

American Maltese Association
2523 N. Starr Street
Tacoma, WA 98403-2940
www.americanmaltese.org

American Kennel Club (AKC)
5580 Centerview Drive
Raleigh, NC 27606-3390
http://www.akc.org

Canadian Kennel Club
89 Skyway Avenue, Suite 100
Etobicoke, Ontario M9W 6R4
Canada

Canine Health Foundation
http://akcchf.org

Other National All-Breed Clubs
http://henceforths.com/kennel_clubs.html

Health-Related Organizations

American Veterinary Medical Association
   (AVMA)
930 North Meacham Road
Schaumburg, IL 60173
www.avma.org

Canine Eye Registration Foundation (CERF)
South Campus Court, Building C
West Lafayette, IN 47907

National Animal Poison Control Center
(NAPCC)
1717 South Philo Road, Suite 36
Urbana, IL 61802
(888) 4ANI-HELP
(888) 426-4435
(900) 680-0000
(Consultation fees apply; call for details)

Orthopedic Foundation for Animals
2300 Nifong Boulevard
Coumbia, MO 65201
http://www.offa.org

Therapy Dogs International
88 Bartley Road
Flanders, NJ 07836
http://www-tdi-dog.org

Rescue

AMA Rescue
46 Maple Village Court
Bernardsville, NJ 07924

The well-bred Maltese is the product of a breeding program administered by a breeder well-versed in Maltese genetics, health, temperament, and conformation.

The evidence is clear: Spayed and neutered Maltese make better pets because they are more focused on their families than they are on other dogs.

Periodicals

Dog World/Dog Fancy Magazines
3 Burroughs
Irvine, CA 92618-2804
www.dogworldmag.com
www.Dogfancy.com

Topnotch Toys
8848 Beverly Hills
Lakeland, FL 33809-1604
(863) 858-3839

The Maltese Rx
Suzanne Johnston, Editor
1970 Rockbrook Court
Fort Worth, Texas 76112

Books

The Complete Dog Book. Official Publication of The American Kennel Club. New York, NY: Howell Book House, 1997.

Abbott, Vicki. *The Maltese, Diminutive Aristocrat*. Hoboken, NJ: Howell Book House, 2000.

Fox, Sue and Armin Kriechbaumer. *Small Dogs*. Hauppauge, NY: Barron's Educational Series, Inc., 2005.

James, Brandlyn. *Guide to Owning a Maltese*. Neptune City, NJ: TFH Publications, 1996.

Videos

AKC Breed Standard Video
http://www.akc.org/store/

About the Authors

Joe Fulda was, for many years, one of America's most respected canine authorities. A distinguished member of the Dog Writers Association of America, he was happiest when he could help others learn more about dogs or how to better care for their dogs. Joe Fulda had a special affection for the toy breeds and his fondness for the little ones is reflected in this tribute to the Maltese.

Betsy Sikora Siino is an award-winning author who has written hundreds of articles and more than two dozen books on animals and their care. Having herself been raised by Maltese, some of her fondest memories include sneaking these adorable dogs into restaurants, airports, ski resorts, hotels, shopping malls, and wherever else dogs were allegedly not allowed.

Acknowledgments

I'd like to express my gratitude to Bev Passe of House of Myi Maltese in Gig Harbor, Washington, for her assistance in educating me about Maltese, for her insight into the breed, and for her photographs and illustrations. Over the past twenty years, I have been fortunate to have seen and judged beautiful Maltese from the House of Myi. My appreciation also goes to Pam Armstrong, fellow Tacoma Kennel Club member and breeder/owner/exhibitor of some very fine Maltese, who provided some wonderful photos. And special thanks to my wife, Mycki, who wouldn't let me stop writing.

Important Note

This pet owner's manual tells the reader how to buy or adopt, and care for a Maltese. The author and publisher consider it important to point out that the advice given in the book is meant primarily for normally developed dogs of excellent physical health and sound temperament.

Anyone who acquires a fully-grown dog should be aware that the animal has already formed its basic impressions of human beings. The new owner should watch the animal carefully, including its behavior toward humans, and, whenever possible, should meet the previous owner.

Caution is further advised in the association of children with dogs, in meeting with other dogs, and in exercising the dog without a leash.

Even well-behaved and carefully supervised dogs sometimes do damage to someone else's property or cause accidents. It is therefore in the owner's interest to be adequately insured against such eventualities, and we strongly urge all dog owners to purchase a liability policy that covers their dog.

Cover Photos

Tara Darling: front cover and back cover; Isabelle Francais: inside front cover and inside back cover.

Photo Credits

Norvia Behling: 9, 17 (bottom), 18, 27, 31, 50, 52 (top), 56, 59, 75; Kent Dannen: 11 (bottom), 17 (top), 21, 22, 23, 25, 32 (top), 34, 36, 37, 41, 45, 57, 61, 62 (bottom), 65, 69, 71, 73, 81, 82, 84, 86, 89, 92; Tara Darling: 2-3, 5, 7, 12 (top left and right and bottom), 15, 24, 38, 42, 44, 47, 58, 62 (top), 63, 64, 74, 76, 77, 79, 80, 83, 93; Isabelle Francais: 4, 11 (top), 14, 20, 28, 39, 43, 48, 51, 52 (bottom), 53, 55, 68, 70, Pets by Paulette: 10, 13, 16, 32 (bottom), 46.

All inquiries should be addressed to:
Barron's Educational Series, Inc.
250 Wireless Boulevard
Hauppauge, NY 11788
www.barronseduc.com

ISBN-13: 978-0-7641-2850-9
ISBN-10: 0-7641-2850-7

Library of Congress Control No. 2005050026

Library of Congress Cataloging-in-Publication Data
Fulda, Joe.
   Maltese: everything about purchase, care, nutrition, behavior, and training / Joe Fulda and Betsy Sikora Siino ; illustrations by Michele Earle-Bridges.
      p. cm.
   Includes index.
   ISBN-13: 978-0-7641-2850-9
   ISBN-10: 0-7641-2850-7
      1. Maltese dog. I. Siino, Betsy Sikora. II. Title.

SF429.M25F85   2006
636.76—dc22   2005050026

Printed in China
9 8 7 6 5 4 3 2 1